Happy B ...
To a great cook, fabulous
friend & beautiful
sister-in-law

COUNTY
HEIRLOOMS

RECIPES & REFLECTIONS FROM PRINCE EDWARD COUNTY

NATALIE WOLLENBERG **&** LEIGH NASH

Invisible Publishing
Halifax & Prince Edward County

Edited by Leigh Nash and Natalie Wollenberg
Production assistance by Andrew Faulkner
Cover and interior photos by Natalie Wollenberg
Food styling by Ruth Gangbar
Cover and interior design by Megan Fildes
With thanks to type designer Rod McDonald

Library and Archives Canada Cataloguing in Publication

Title: County heirlooms / edited by Natalie Wollenberg & Leigh Nash.
Names: Wollenberg, Natalie, 1977- editor. | Nash, Leigh, 1982- editor.

Identifiers:
Canadiana (print) 20200228439 | Canadiana (ebook) 20200229028
ISBN 9781988784519 (softcover) | ISBN 9781988784601 (HTML)

Subjects:
LCSH: Cooking—Ontario—Prince Edward. | LCSH: Local foods—Ontario—Prince Edward. | LCSH: Cooks—Ontario—Prince Edward—Anecdotes. | LCSH: Farmers—Ontario—Prince Edward—Anecdotes. | LCSH: Food industry and trade—Ontario—Prince Edward—Anecdotes. | LCGFT: Cookbooks. | LCGFT: Anecdotes.

Classification: LCC TX715.6 C68 2020 | DDC 641.59713/587—dc23

Invisible Publishing | Halifax & Prince Edward County
www.invisiblepublishing.com

Printed and bound in Canada

We acknowledge for their financial support of our publishing program the Canada Council for the Arts, the Ontario Arts Council, and the Government of Canada.

 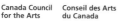  

INTRODUCTION   1

ABOUT THE BOOK   3

AARON ARMSTRONG   4
GRILLED LITTLE GEM ROMAINE   6

CHRIS & JESSIE ARMSTRONG   8
MAPLE HONEY CORNBREAD   10

ANGELA & TIM BAKER   12
BEST BEEF STEW IN EXISTENCE!   14

ANGELO BEAN   16
COCKTAIL DI FAGIOLI E COZZE   18

MICHAEL BELL   20
BACON-WRAPPED MEATBALLS   22

LAURA BORUTSKI & ELLIOT REYNOLDS   24
COUNTY SMOKED HAM   26

CHRIS BYRNE   28
SOCCA FLATBREAD   30

HEATHER COFFEY & STEPHANIE LAING   32
SQUASH RISOTTO   34

NATALIE COMEAU   36
HONEY, LEMON & ROSEMARY VINAIGRETTE   38

JOAQUIM & AMOR CONDE   40
CHANFANA   42

JENIFER DEAN   44
HARD CIDER CHEDDAR DIP   46

NEIL DOWSON   48
BEEF & ALE PIE   50

VICKI EMLAW   52
PANZANELLA   54

JENNA EMPEY   56
DILL & GARLIC SAUERKRAUT   58

ANDREAS FELLER 60
QUICHE LORRAINE 62

MIKE FOUNTOUKIS 64
BAKLAVA 66

RUTH GANGBAR 68
CARROT & TRIPLE-CHOCOLATE CUPCAKES 70

ENID GRACE 72
SPINACH & RICOTTA GNUDI WITH HERB BUTTER SAUCE 74

LEAH MARSHALL HANNON 78
PICKEREL CAKES WITH FANCY
TARTAR SAUCE & FENNEL SLAW 80

JARED HARTLEY 84
MOUSSE DE FOIE 86

REBECCA HUNT 88
MEZZE PLATTER 90

LEE ARDEN LEWIS 94
SUMAC BAKED BANNOCK & MOHAWK LYED CORN SOUP 96

LUHANA & ZACH LITTLEJOHN 100
COCKEREL COOKED IN SHERRY CREAM 102

SAS LONG 104
FLOURLESS CHOCOLATE CAKE 106

JENNIFER MCCAW 108
BLUEBERRY SHORTCAKES 110

GAVIN NORTH & BAY WOODYARD 112
HAZELNUT HONEY BUCKWHEAT BROWNIES 114

TIM NOXON 116
LEFTOVER PRIME RIB & LENTIL SOUP 118

ALBERT PONZO 120
FRENCH-STYLE OMELETTE 122

MICHAEL POTTERS 124
CONIGLIO WITH PEPPERONATA & SAUCE DIABLE 126

STEVE PURTELLE   130
BLUE CHEESE DRESSING   132

SCOTT ROYCE   134
SPARKLING RASPBERRY GELÉE   136

NICHOLAS SORBARA   138
BEAN BALLS   140

LILI SULLIVAN   142
CHICKEN & ASPARAGUS TERRINE   144

MICHAEL SULLIVAN   146
STEAK TARTARE   148

GLENN SYMONS   150
HARVEST CHOUCROUTE   152

ED & SANDI TAYLOR   154
KOHLRABI & CARROT SLAW   156

SAMANTHA VALDIVIA   158
CHILES RELLENOS   160

BRIAN & JANE WALT   162
ROSEMARY MAPLE GLAZED NUTS   164

HENRY WILLIS   166
RAISIN RYE FRENCH TOAST BAKE   168

NATALIE WOLLENBERG   170
**PUTTANESCA SAUCE WITH
ROASTED EGGPLANT**   172

CHRIS WYLIE   174
CURRIED CARROT GINGER SOUP   176

HIDDE ZOMER   178
WOOD-FIRED BELGIAN ENDIVE   180

ACKNOWLEDGEMENTS   185

Introduction

I've always been interested in stories of how people arrived in Prince Edward County, Ontario: where they've come from, why they decided to stay, and why they're still here now. How did they grow up, and how did they get into cooking (or farming, or bee-keeping, or maple sugaring)? What have they learned along the way? What drives them to keep going? What's next? ¶ The idea for *County Heirlooms* came from being lucky enough to be submerged into the County's hospitality industry. It's a tight-knit group; our farmers, food producers, and chefs work closely together. And we're lucky to live in a place where farm produce is so accessible. It's nothing out of the ordinary to go to a local restaurant and see a farmer dropping off produce and talking to a chef about what's going to be available in the weeks to come. But even in a place where food is so accessible, there are still community members who experience food insecurity as part of their daily lives. ¶ I became involved with Food to Share after pouring beer at their yearly charity event, during which a local chef cooked for 120 people. Volunteers served beer, wine, and a three-course meal made from locally donated produce. It was inspiring to see so many people come together to try and improve local food security. ¶ Food to Share's concept is simple: use locally grown food to produce prepared meals that can be distributed through food banks and community groups. As part of Food to Share's regular programming, twice every week, volunteers come together in a community kitchen and cook 120 fresh meals for local food banks. ¶ Seeing all of this work, and the continued need for it, I wanted to do something more. All royalties from sales of *County Heirlooms* will go to support Food to Share's ongoing programming. ¶ I hope you learn something new from these interviews, or are inspired to try a new recipe and share it with someone, or to volunteer in your local community.

—Natalie Wollenberg

About the Book

These interviews and recipes showcase the talent and creativity we're lucky to have here in Prince Edward County. ¶ We envisioned this book as a really excellent dinner party, where each "guest" was invited to talk a little bit about why they do what they do, and to bring a recipe to share. To stay faithful to this vision, we tried our best during the editorial process to keep each recipe true to the contributor's voice. The result is an eclectic presentation: some recipes have headnotes, some have numerous variations/permutations, some have clear plating instructions. Others are more open to interpretation. ¶ We've included the names of the organizations that contributors are affiliated with at the time of the book's publication, but this project is intended to be a celebration of local people and their work, rather than a traditional guidebook. ¶ We hope you'll try making some of these recipes, and we encourage you to find ways to make them your own. And we also hope this book inspires you, wherever you live, to find personal ways to connect with local growers, chefs, and makers—and, of course, your food.

—Leigh Nash

Aaron Armstrong

Farmer, Blue Wheelbarrow Farm
Aaron has been working in the field (literally) of organic vegetable farming since 2010.

I had three moments when I knew I wanted to go into farming. In kindergarten, my teacher asked the class to paint what we wanted to be when we grew up. Others kids picked super-unrealistic careers like astronaut or explorer. And I picked being a farmer. Which is just like the unrealistic ones in that it won't make you any money, but you'll love doing it. Then, after school, I travelled around Europe working on farms. In Greece, a farmhand told me, "You're going to make a good farmer one day." I'd never actually thought of farming as a living before that moment. Later that year, I was on a farm in Devon, England. That's where I worked my first farmers' market. It was my first time talking with people about vegetables, and I had no idea how to speak about food and about growing. But seeing our stand clear out was amazing. There was an incredible energy, the whole place was buzzing with vitality. At that moment, I was hooked—that's when I decided to make farming my career. ¶ I discovered Prince Edward County in 2014, when I moved here to work at Fiddlehead Farm. And April 2016 is when I purchased my property, during my seventh year of farming. I'd spent years hopping around and I wasn't in a place for more than six months at a time. I loved it. It was great. But with the County I thought, "Oh my God, I can see myself here long-term." ¶ Because it's a short growing season in Ontario, all my income happens in five months. The only part of this job I hate is when I'm not farming in the wintertime. It's so quiet and I have to get other work for a few months. ¶ I love my spreadsheets. I used to work at a toy company, and that's where I learned Excel. It's an invaluable skill for me in planning what I grow. ¶ The Hubb (at Angeline's) was the first restaurant I delivered to on my very first harvest day. They were really impressed by the longevity of the greens, how fresh they stayed. Which is exactly what I wanted them to do. The next year, I was a small plate on their menu. They showed me the menu, and there was a dish called Aaron's Greens. It was the first time I'd ever been featured. That relationship with Laura and Elliot (now the proprietors of the Bloomfield Public House Market) has been a real catalyst for me. ¶ I'm so lucky I found this place. Every failure and success in my life led me to owning a farm in Prince Edward County. There are no wasted experiences in my past because all of them brought me here.

GRILLED LITTLE GEM ROMAINE

4 Little Gem or baby romaine lettuce heads

2 tbsp olive oil, for brushing

1 lemon, juiced

coarse salt

Parmesan cheese

pepper to taste

Heat grill or barbecue to medium-high heat.

Slice romaine heads in half lengthwise, keeping the cores intact. Rinse out the centre of each head to flush out any dirt or grit.

Brush both sides of each romaine half with olive oil.

Grill lettuces for 2 minutes each side, or until the leaves become lightly charred.

Plate the lettuces cut side up and dress with fresh lemon juice, salt, grated Parmesan cheese, and pepper.

Chris & Jessie Armstrong

Farmers, LOHA Farms

A family-driven hobby farm that teaches visitors about animals, bees & farm life.

We both grew up here, met in high school, and left for work. We moved back to Prince Edward County in 2009 after we had kids, and bought the farm down the road in 2012. ¶ Shortly after buying the property, we decided to get some animals, and we now have goats, pigs, chickens, and ducks. We named the farm LOHA after our kids (Leah, Oaklie, Hannah, and Asher), because they're the reason we got into farming. No one in our family has any background in farming. This all started as a hobby, because we like being outside and working with our hands. ¶ Five years ago, we started maple syrup. We figured we should enjoy our maple trees. But we had no clue what we were doing—we just crossed our fingers and hoped it worked. Now we produce about 500 litres of maple syrup, and we're involved in Maple in the County, which draws thousands of tourists to the County every March. ¶ We do everything the old-fashioned way, so it takes forever. We're up all night, for an entire month. At some points, it's around-the-clock shifts of just throwing wood on the fire. It's a long process, but we enjoy it. ¶ We first became interested in bees after a friend asked to put a couple hives on our property. And that sparked something. Now we have over thirty hives, with hopes of expanding. We're fortunate to have 130 acres, which means we can have a bunch of different locations for beehives, which all produce different flavours. ¶ We also have a few ponds that we play hockey on in the winter. Every year, we excavate them a little bit more to turn them into little estuaries. Slowly, we're hooking them up together. Eventually, we'll have a canal system so people can skate from pond to pond. Our goal is to show our kids everything farm life has to offer, and to have some fun while doing so.

MAPLE HONEY CORNBREAD

1 cup yellow cornmeal

1 cup all-purpose flour

1 tbsp baking powder

1 tsp salt

¼ cup unsalted butter, melted and cooled slightly

½ cup maple syrup

¼ cup honey

2 eggs, lightly beaten

1 cup milk

Preheat oven to 400°F. Place a medium-sized cast-iron skillet in the oven (or grease an 8-inch square baking pan and line with parchment paper).

In a large bowl, mix the cornmeal, flour, baking powder, and salt.

Make a well in the dry ingredients and add the butter, maple syrup, honey, eggs, and milk. Stir to combine, being careful not to overmix.

Remove cast-iron skillet from oven; add enough olive oil to coat bottom. Scrape batter into hot skillet (or into prepared baking pan); smooth top.

Bake for 20 to 25 minutes, or until golden brown on edges, and a toothpick comes out clean when pressed into centre. Best served warm.

Angela & Tim Baker

Farmers, Jubilee Forest Farm
A family-owned, pasture-based farm built on & run with regenerative farming principles.

Both of us grew up here. After our oldest daughter was born, we bought a piece of property. That same year, we watched the documentary *Food Inc*. And it changed us. ¶ We started to read Joel's Salatin's books *Family Friendly Farming* and *You Can Farm*. And we thought, "Yes, that's the life we want for our family." ¶ We did too much at the beginning. It's good to be a diversified farm because all the different elements work together. But we went too far. It was too much, too fast. ¶ To do it right, we needed to heal the land before we started growing the grains. If your soil is dependent on fertilizer, you can't just switch to organic farming. You have to put organic matter back into the soil, make it healthy again. ¶ We started by moving our cows into a new pasture every single day. In nature, cows are never tomorrow where they work today. It's the quickest way to bring life back into the soil. What we didn't realize is how much carbon that actually draws down from the atmosphere and puts into the soil. If you build the right system, you'll have a sustainable, regenerative succession forward as opposed to a regression system on the soil. Beef are a big part of the problem, but managed properly, they can be a solution to our climate problem. Basically, it's not the cow, it's the how. ¶ We also have our laying hens follow our cows to scratch the cow patties. And they eat the bugs and sanitize the pasture. ¶ We built an egg mobile for our hens. It's an old camper trailer; we gutted it and installed nesting boxes and a slatted mesh floor. So at night, all the manure drops right to the floor, onto the pasture where you want it. And we don't have to muck it out. After one day of training, they all learned to go back inside it at night. And once it gets dark, we just close the little doggy door on it, and in the morning, hook it up to the tractor and move it to a new section of the pasture, and open up the door. At night they all come back inside because that's where they roost. That's where they lay their eggs. ¶ In the perfect system, we need grain farmers and cattle farmers sharing their land so that cattle can run on land to heal and restore it, and then switch back and forth so you can use that healed land to grow grains to feed chickens and pigs—and people. ¶ We raised 1,200 meat birds this year. So we got in the artisanal chicken program, and we can keep growing until we raise 3,000 a year. And then after that we'll apply to be in what's called the niche market program, which is up from 6,000 to 20,000. And we can do it all out on pasture. ¶ Eating what's around you is my idea of a solution. Can you imagine if the whole world started eating locally, even in the wintertime? Sure, we change our diet slightly in the winter. We eat more root veggies, we're not eating fresh lettuce and tomatoes when it's cold out, but they'll come again next summer. ¶ It takes just as much work, if not more, to market your product than to grow it and produce it. When you're a direct-market farmer, selling at markets and local events lets you avoid the middleman so that you can actually make a living farming. And people can feel really good about purchasing products from farmers like us.

BEST BEEF STEW IN EXISTENCE!

1½ lbs Jubilee stew beef

1 tbsp olive oil

1 tsp salt

1 tsp pepper

1 tsp Italian seasoning

2½ cups beef bone broth

2 tbsp Worcestershire sauce

3 garlic cloves, minced

1 large onion, chopped

4 large carrots, chopped

1 lb potatoes, cubed

1 cup tomato sauce

2 tbsp organic cornstarch

2 tbsp water

fresh parsley, for garnish

The veggies for this recipe come from our winter CSA box through Fiddlehead Farm.

This is our current favourite recipe. We use an Instant Pot, which makes things super quick and easy—and delicious!

Add the olive oil to an Instant Pot and turn on the sauté function. When the oil starts to sizzle, add the meat and season with the salt, pepper, and Italian seasoning.

Cook the meat until browned on all sides. Add the beef broth to the Instant Pot and use a spoon to scrape the brown bits from the bottom of the pan.

Add the Worcestershire sauce, garlic, onion, carrots, potatoes, and tomato sauce. Close the lid and steam valve on the Instant Pot.

Cook on high pressure for 35 minutes, then allow the pressure to release naturally for 10 minutes before doing a quick release.

Mix together the cornstarch and cold water in a small bowl and stir into the stew until thickened.

Serve topped with finely chopped parsley and crusty bread.

Angelo Bean

Artisan Sausage Maker/Instructor

In his Italian Cooking Studio, Angelo shares time-honoured methods of handmade cooking in a creative atmosphere where food, music, conversation & wine all come to play.

Why am I in the County? It's got to do with wine. I worked as a cabinetmaker for about thirty years, and wine was my hobby. I've been a wine lover all my life. For the last sixteen years of my professional life, I was a product consultant with the LCBO. Seven years ago, while tasting wines at the LCBO tasting lab, Billy Munnelly, a wine writer who owns property in Cherry Valley, suggested I retire in the County. He said, "You'll fit right in." Intrigued, my wife and I drove out that weekend. Within a year, we bought a beautiful treed lot with the perfect house. ¶ I'm Italian—we make wines, we preserve tomatoes, we make sausages. I didn't learn how to make sausages anywhere in particular, it's just something my family always did. I was born into it. ¶ In Toronto, my sausages were featured in some of the best shops and got plenty of media coverage. When I first moved out to the County, I started using local wines to produce the wine-infused sausages I'd made in Toronto. They were an immediate hit. It's still a joy to go around the County and have people recognize me as the County sausage maker. ¶ For five years, I painstakingly renovated our house in the County, transforming it into the Angelo Bean Italian Cooking Studio. My classes took off as soon as I put up the schedule online. ¶ My cooking studio has become my new passion. The classes are all totally interactive and hands-on. I teach traditional methods of regional cooking using vintage tools. We work together the old-fashioned way—everything is done by hand and guided by the heart. People come to my home studio for an original, unique experience. ¶ I'm having fun and following my own rules. Whatever I use has to be local or organic or free-range. I purchase class ingredients mindfully. I want to know where they come from. ¶ All the dishware we use is made entirely by hand by a County artisan. All the decor and cooking tools in the Studio have a story. ¶ One of my favourite classes I do now is a five-course tasting menu. All the recipes we make are mine. They are my creations based on memories of my mother's cooking, with the addition of my wine- and spirit-infused techniques.

COCKTAIL DI FAGIOLI E COZZE

Pasta and beans with mussels is a popular soup in Naples. My version has no pasta, uses cannellini beans, and is served in a martini glass. The bean soup base can be made conveniently in advance and finished with seafood when you're ready to serve it.

1 small shallot, finely minced

1 garlic clove, peeled and lightly crushed

3 tbsp olive oil

3½ oz smoked bacon (or pancetta or guanciale), finely chopped

½ cup each finely chopped carrot and celery

1–2 whole fresh peperoncino hot pepper, seeded and sliced (optional)

a few dashes white wine, for sautéing beans and steaming mussels

1 can (398 ml) cannellini beans, drained and rinsed*

2 cans (284 ml) chicken or seafood stock (or about 2⅓ cups homemade stock)**

1 lb fresh mussels***

1 tsp grated lemon zest

2 parsley sprigs, stemmed and chopped

pinch each finely minced fresh rosemary, thyme, and sage

splash Sambuca

kosher salt and black pepper to taste

lemon wedges, for serving

In a saucepan, gently sauté the shallot and garlic in 1 tablespoon olive oil. When golden, discard the garlic. Add the bacon, carrot, celery, and peperoncino (if using).

Gently sauté, adding a little white wine in the process to help soften the vegetables and to deglaze the pan. The aromas emerging as you sauté should drive you mad with anticipation! Add the cannellini beans and stock; reduce over medium heat until broth is creamy, or for about 10 minutes. At this point, you can refrigerate the soup if making ahead.

Rinse mussels in a colander under cold water and discard any opened ones. In a large pot with a lid, bring a little white wine to a boil. (You don't want to drown the mussels; just add enough liquid to create steam). Add the mussels and cover, stirring occasionally, until they're all opened.

Reserve some whole mussels in their shells for garnish. Discard remaining shells and place all mussels into a bowl with their own broth, along with 1 tablespoon olive oil, lemon zest, and parsley (refrigerate if making ahead).

To serve, drain the seafood from its broth. Reheat the bean mixture, drained mussels, minced herbs, Sambuca, and just enough mussel broth to give the soup flavour without diluting it too much. Season with salt and pepper to taste.

Divide the bean mixture into serving glasses; top each with reserved shell-on mussels, a squirt of lemon juice, and a little additional olive oil and lemon zest.

*Using dried beans is best, but you need to soak them in water overnight, and then cover with fresh water before cooking until tender. Use about 2¼ cups of cooked beans (made from about 1 cup dried beans) to substitute canned beans.

**Stock is important. I usually make my own and store it frozen. You can buy premade ones in specialty shops. Avoid the boxed ones in supermarkets.

***You can find 1 lb bags of fresh PEI mussels in most supermarkets. Feel free to add about ½ lb clams or shrimp to this recipe. Avoid the canned stuff as it does not taste good.

Michael Bell

Chef, Big Mike's BBQ

A central Texas barbecue-inspired food truck that uses real woodsmoke to handcraft meat.

When I was seven or eight, my dad taught me how to fry an egg—and I was completely hooked. I was the oldest kid in the house, so I was in charge of making lunches. And once I started making lunches, I figured I'd make a dinner once in a while. ¶ My grandmother taught my dad how to bake because he'd finish off the pan of brownies all on his own. He's not a small man either. And she was just so tired of making these pans of disappearing date squares and brownies. It was kind of the same deal for me. My nana—my mom's mom—still has her recipe, the Tenderflake cookie recipe for chocolate chip cookies. They were my favourite thing to eat. So, as soon as I could learn to bake, I made that recipe. And then I ended up entering them in the fair one year and won a ribbon at the Picton Fair. So then it was like, all right, I guess I like cooking. I like baking. ¶ My first job was a high school co-op placement at the Waring House. I started culinary school at Loyalist College and moved to North Bay to finish my education at Canadore College. And that's when I bought myself a Weber charcoal barbecue. ¶ I hosted a lot of parties, and I got sick and tired of people getting hungry at midnight and ordering cardboard crap pizza. So I started buying giant pork shoulders and throwing them on the smoker all day. I played around with making pulled pork on a charcoal Weber for five or six years. ¶ When I moved home to the County, somebody said, "You make really good pulled pork. You should try a brisket." So I did, and it was absolutely awful. It took me a while before my brisket was reasonably good, because that kind of meat can be really challenging. ¶ Somebody gave me a book called *The Prophets of Smoked Meat*, about barbecue in Texas. In the central Texas tradition, you only use salt and pepper, and you cook everything in a pit with flame and wood. No chips, no charcoal. As a classically trained chef, it resonated with me, the fact that I can take a piece of meat, put salt and pepper on it, and then all the magic happens because I watch over it with a wood fire. I'm no longer chained to a stove or a deep fryer or convection oven. Now, that being said, I stand beside a fire that is as hot as the mouth of hell. But I really enjoy it. I get a suntan now. ¶ Running a barbecue business can be tricky, because there are certain cuts—the ribs, for instance—that aren't really the best to serve the next day. And I want to serve the highest quality barbecue every single time. ¶ Everything needs to stand on its own on a plate. It's great to have the best brisket. But the coleslaw better match it. The beans better be just as good. The cornbread has to taste just as good as the rest of the stuff on the plate. ¶ The back of my car is jam-packed with peppers and onions and cabbage and carrots. And it's grown right here in the County. That's important to me because my family is a farming family. ¶ When I see a platter come back to me and there's not a stitch of food left on it, and the customer is still trying to pick up the crumbs as they pass it back to me—that's when I've done my job properly.

BACON-WRAPPED MEATBALLS

2½ lbs ground chuck

2 eggs

1 cup seasoned bread crumbs

1 cup crispy fried onions
(French's or other)

¼ cup Big Mike's sauce
(or ketchup)

1 tbsp chili powder

1 tbsp salt

1 tbsp pepper

a few dashes of your
favourite hot sauce

Preheat smoker to 250°F. Mike suggests using maple to smoke the meatballs.

Mix all ingredients together in a bowl until spices and crispy onions are evenly distributed and the bowl is clean. You should be able to make one giant meatball with the mix.

Portion meatballs using a 2 oz scoop or by hand to make 24 equal balls.

Cut strips of bacon in half and wrap each ball. Roll between hands to form the bacon to the shape.

Place in small roasting pan. Chill in the refrigerator unwrapped for 2 hours to set.

Smoke meatballs for 2 hours at 250°F or until they have reached an internal temperature of 170°F.

Serve with Big Mike's sauce.

> No need for a smoker if you don't have one: prepare the recipe in the same fashion, and roast the meatballs in an oven preheated to 350°F for 30 to 45 minutes or until they reach an internal temperature of 170°F.

Laura Borutski & Elliot Reynolds

Owners, Bloomfield Public House Market

A farm-to-table gastropub turned grocery market & Southern pit barbecue.

For our first business in Prince Edward County, we were the Wiener Smiths. We found a hot dog cart on Kijiji, and we started off at the Hayloft. We ran that for three years, on weekends after working our full-time jobs. ¶ The Fidas approached us to see if we wanted to take over the restaurant space at Angeline's. It was a great partnership but big shoes to fill, because everybody who had gone to Angeline's had all these beautiful stories of Willie and Monica and how Angeline's used to be. ¶ With The Hubb, we tried to introduce more of a casual style to dining, while keeping the emphasis on food done really, really well. It was a huge growing experience. ¶ It was a lot of work, and after five years, we decided to take a break. But as much as we say we wanted to take a year off, we knew we'd never take a year off. After a couple of weeks, the opportunity to purchase the old CIBC building in Bloomfield came up. We bought it, and started work on the Bloomfield Public House. ¶ We wanted to make it a neighbourhood spot. Which is tough because we come from a higher-end restaurant background. But that's the beauty of it: really great things, but done in an approachable way. We sat downstairs for weeks trying to map out what it was going to look like. But it was really thinking about what Bloomfield didn't have: coffee. So let's do coffee. Wow—that was a learning curve. A long bar is something we've always wanted. An open kitchen. It took five weeks of gutting until we could truly see the building's potential. ¶ Charcuterie's always been a big thing for us. We do all our stuff in-house, and that sets us apart. So that's how that part of the menu started. With Elliot's food, it's about textures and flavours on a plate. There's gonna be something pickley, something crunchy, savoury—it always has a lot of texture to it. ¶ At the root of everything, we're celebrating our friends who are farmers down the road by using their great products. Blue Wheelbarrow has amazing lettuces, so they're going on the menu. Hagerman has some great broccoli. Let's get in the truck and go get some broccoli and put it on the menu. That's as simple as it gets. Yes, we can't do that year-round. But when we can do it, let's do it. People come down here to experience the County, so let's showcase it. ¶ In 2020, we decided to shift our space. Now it's the Bloomfield Public House Market, and we sell local produce and prepared food. It's fitting, because the building was originally built to be a grocery store named Judy's. We also decided to launch the County's first Southern fried chicken and barbecue pit, fittingly named Judy's Fried Chicken & Barbecue. It's exciting to bring the past and future together in one place.

COUNTY SMOKED HAM

This is a multi-step recipe that includes time needed for brining, drying, and smoking. Various cuts of pork can be used for this recipe, but we prefer to use the sirloin tip, which is the smallest cut of the three-piece pork leg. We use this cut because when it's finished, it resembles the classic ham shape we all know.

Ham

1 piece about 4–5 lbs pork sirloin tip (coppa/loin works nicely in this recipe as well)

1 piece meat netting roll, size 18 or 22 (try asking your butcher to supply 12"–15" or order from a specialty butcher supplier online)

smoker, either wood-fired or use wood chips

Brine

4 L water

2 cups salt

2 cups sugar

¼ cup + 1 tbsp molasses

¼ cup cure #1 or pink curing salt

2 tbsp black pepper, ground

1 tbsp celery seed

½ tsp allspice, ground

1 bay leaf, crushed

Glaze

2 cups cranberries, frozen

1 cup molasses

2 tbsp sherry vinegar

2 tbsp black pepper

salt to taste

Bring the brine to a boil and remove from heat. Allow brine to chill completely, then pour it into a non-reactive container (plastic is best). Place the sirloin tip in the brine and keep it fully submerged for 6 days.

Take the pork out of the brine and pat dry. Stuff the sirloin tip into the ham netting, and twist and tie it until tight. Knot it off and place on a rack in the refrigerator to dry overnight.

Preheat your smoker before you put the ham in; we recommend holding a constant temperature between 175°F and 225°F. Hot smoke your ham for 6 to 8 hours or until it reaches an internal temperature of 165°F.

Prepare the glaze by combining all the ingredients in a sauce pot. Bring the mixture to a boil, then reduce to a simmer for 5 minutes. Remove from heat and allow to cool. Purée using an immersion blender or food processor, then strain and reserve for glazing the ham during smoking.

Throughout the smoking process we glaze the ham. This results in a richer, darker colour and imparts a delicious complementary finish.

When the ham is finished, cool down completely and enjoy!

We recommend snacking on it with mustard or serving it sliced, drizzled with a little browned butter, and garnished with aged cheddar and finely chopped chives.

Chris Byrne

Vegan Chef

Chef Chris offers gourmet vegetarian, vegan & raw-inspired catering.

I grew up in Belleville, Ontario. I had my first vegetarian meal at the Naam, a twenty-four-hour vegetarian restaurant in Vancouver that's been around since the 1960s. I had home fries with miso gravy, and it was so good. I became a vegetarian very soon after that, and it kind of freaked everyone out. My friends told me, "We'd hang out with you, but we don't know what to serve you." So I said, "Invite me over and I'll cook." That's how I got started as a chef. ¶ I ran into the idea of macrobiotics, cooking with the seasons, working with ferments and wild foods. Eventually, I quit my ad executive job to work on organic farms. The whole time I studied macrobiotic cooking. I wrote an essay to my hero, Cornelia Aihara. She was the best macrobiotic chef, and she and her husband, Herman (who was a philosopher), ran the Vega Institute in Chico, California. They invited me to stay with them for a year, and I shadowed her, learning all about Japanese folk foods. I learned about making soy sauce, miso, and pickles—the foundations of Japanese cuisine. ¶ Following that, I moved to Toronto. Fressen was opening, and it was Canada's first gourmet vegan restaurant. I became the sous-chef there, and worked there for years, developing many dishes and plating techniques. It was so inspiring. ¶ I spent years catering on Vancouver Island, and then decided to move back to the County to be near family. I saw a culinary scene developing here that I felt I could engage with. Then vegan food had this renaissance, and I thought, "This is my moment." ¶ I think people in the County have always been interested in using local fare. But in the last decade, the production of intriguing food has really come a long way. It always inspires my creativity. ¶ My big focus these days is wild foods. My wife's an herbalist and we live on a farm where we let lots of wild plants grow. When harvested and prepared properly, these wild foods are unique, delicious, packed with nutrition, and a celebration of our wonderful home, Prince Edward County.

SOCCA FLATBREAD

Flatbread

2 cups chickpea flour

½ tsp salt

2 cups water

1 tbsp olive oil

2 tbsp sunflower oil

Sauce

4 tbsp tahini

1 tbsp white wine vinegar

1 tsp salt

About 3 tbsp water (amount varies based on texture of tahini)

Toppings

1 tbsp olive oil

2 garlic cloves, minced

1 leek, sliced thinly

1 cup mushrooms of your choice, sliced

4 stalks rapini, sliced into 1" segments

1 tbsp lemon juice

Additional topping suggestions include dollops of tomato sauce, pesto, artichoke hearts, diced sweet peppers, grilled zucchini, sun-dried tomatoes, or your favourite in-season veggies or herbs.

To prepare the flatbread, preheat oven to 425°F. Place two 9-inch cast-iron pans into oven. Mix chickpea flour and salt together. Whisk in water until there are no lumps; stir in olive oil. Remove pans from oven, add sunflower oil, and place back in oven for 1 minute. Remove pans again and add enough batter to cover the bottom of both pans; swirl around as if you are making a crepe. Place in oven for 10 minutes.

To prepare the sauce, mix all ingredients together. Add water and stir vigorously until sauce comes together. It should be smooth and the texture of a cream sauce. Spread evenly over flatbread.

To prepare the toppings, in skillet, sauté garlic in oil over medium heat. Add leeks and cook until wilted. Add mushrooms and cook until soft. Add rapini and lemon juice; cook for an additional 15 seconds.

Spread toppings on sauced flatbread and put back into oven for 5 minutes or until toppings are cooked to desired effect. Serves 4. Enjoy!

Heather Coffey & Stephanie Laing

Farmers, Fiddlehead Farm

A small-scale organic farm feeding over 200 farm-share families & supplying restaurants.

We moved to the County in June 2012. We originally bought this house on a whim. We'd never been to the County, and had just recently started dating. Partially, what got us into this was a love of food and wine. ¶ The first year we started the farm, we had all the up-front investments, and we lost $40,000. The second year, we bounced back and were able to actually make some money, but it wasn't enough to live off. And then slowly, every year, we invested money back in to build the basic infrastructure, to build the capacity we needed to pay the mortgage. ¶ I'd say for us, now in year eight of operations, the farm looks nothing like what we initially thought it would look like. We're just vegetables now, no animals. We were initially washing vegetables underneath a tarp in an old gazebo, until we finally got a grant to build a small cover-all shelter. ¶ The first few years, we sold our produce mostly at farmers' markets because they were low-hanging fruit. But we've got twenty-two weeks where we can actually sell at farmers' markets. And if you miss one, you can't make it up. That's partially why we've shifted to really focused growth on our community-supported agriculture (CSA) program. ¶ In 2019, we decided to finally invest in a CSA service system that allows people to customize their boxes. Because the downside to a lot of CSA models is, especially in our early years, that people were getting whatever we decided to give them. This system that we started in 2018 has really allowed people to tailor their boxes to what they're actually going to be using in the kitchen. They're not getting vegetables that go to waste because they don't eat kohlrabi or beets. ¶ A lot of restaurants use us now. It elevates the story behind the food: does the customer want it to be just a burger or do they want their burger to have a bit more backstory? ¶ Local chefs too want something unique, something hard to get fresh. For us, sometimes it's a challenge; it's like, let's see if we can grow that here. ¶ Maintaining a relationship can be a challenge when you're business partners too, because sometimes you need to have intimate talk time, not just business talk time. The bickering, especially in front of your staff, can be hard. But working together gives you a common bond. ¶ The most rewarding thing is the customers. Those moments with people who appreciate our food re-energize us. We've had some customers for the better part of a decade. We're their farm, and they come to us.

SQUASH RISOTTO

1 squash (approx. 2½ lbs);
like Koginut or other darker,
fuller-flavoured varieties

1 tbsp olive oil

1 large onion, diced

1–3 garlic cloves, finely minced

1 tsp dried sage
(or 1 tbsp fresh sage)

½ cup Parmesan, finely grated
(about 2 oz)

2 cups vegetable or chicken broth

1 cup short-grain rice
(like Arborio)

salt to taste

Roast extra squash halves as bowls for serving the finished risotto, sprinkled with extra Parmesan, sage, and toasted squash seeds.

Cut squash in half and discard seeds (or save for roasting; see below).

Set squash cut-side up into a roasting pan, helping to hold in juices and to caramelize the flesh. Bake at 375°F for 45 to 60 minutes or until softened. Cool slightly.

While squash is cooking, heat olive oil in a high-sided skillet over low heat. Sauté the onions and garlic. Once onions are tender, add rice and stir to toast slightly. While stirring, add broth one ladle-ful at a time; wait until each addition of broth is absorbed before adding more. Cook while stirring often, for about 20 to 30 minutes, or until the rice is creamy and almost tender.

Add spoonfuls of squash to the rice while stirring in the sage and Parmesan. Season with salt to taste before serving. Risotto is best served immediately.

To roast squash seeds (for topping): Rinse seeds in a colander under cold water to remove any squash; drain well. Line a large baking sheet with parchment paper and toss the seeds with enough olive oil to lightly coat. Smooth into an even layer, season with salt to taste, and bake at 375°F for about 15 to 20 minutes or until crispy and golden, stirring several times while cooking.

Natalie Comeau

Beekeeper, The Prince Edward County Honey Company
A small producer of raw, small-batch local honey that highlights the terroir of the County.

When we moved here in 2012, I wanted the big garden, chickens, the whole thing. I hadn't planned on getting bees until I saw an ad from Honey Pie Hives & Herbals about their beekeeping class. I took it in the summer of 2013 and got a hive of my own. And promptly lost my bees, killed my queen, and then had the replacement queen's hive get robbed out by wasps. That first year was a disaster. ¶ I spent the winter learning. I took an online class in bee biology through the University of Guelph, and they let me write my research paper on the effect of terroir on honey. As research, I picked a few areas in the County, looked at the honey plants growing here and the types of honey those plants produced. In theory, different areas would produce different-tasting honey. But after I'd talked to a few local beekeepers, it turned out to be more complicated. ¶ The next winter, I received a grant for field research. I chose five different locations in the County and placed two hives in each. And lo and behold, the honey turned out different in each spot. ¶ One of the locations was Campbell's Orchard, which I left unattended for too long. When we finally extracted honey from the two hives, we noticed one pail was dark and one was light. We extrapolated that the bees from one hive went left and the bees from the other hive went right. It was the perfect illustration for our concept. ¶ Everybody's all about saving bees, which is great. But the bees that really need to be saved are the wild bees that suffer when nobody is out there looking after them. So if you want to save the bees, don't get a hive and then neglect it. Instead, plant flowers. Stop mowing your ditch. Stop using pesticides. ¶ I am really a bit of a data geek. I make notes every time I go out. And so I know this hive has this queen, they produce this much honey. I am still very leery about messing with Mother Nature. Every time we think we've got it, there's so much more that we don't know. But I definitely do notice a difference between bees that have been selected and bees that have not been selected in the biodynamic program. ¶ Some people think selective breeding is part of the problem with bees, that by selectively choosing what we want, we're taking away from the bees and what bees think is important. ¶ Ontario imports huge numbers of queens. So we need young people getting into bees and bee breeding. You know, young people who are into animals and genetics. It's hard, but there's a lot of start-up funding available, especially for young people who want to get involved. ¶ I don't wear big gloves, because then you can feel invincible and it's easy to get sloppy. I use thin medical gloves, which keeps things clean from one hive to another, and they force me to be more conscious of what I'm doing. ¶ I always talk to the bees. I'll open the hive and say, "Hi, girls, how are you today?" It makes a real difference. I think it ties into that old tradition of when the beekeeper dies, somebody has to go and tell the bees. It gets lonely working in the bee yard alone, and talking makes you more conscious of them as little creatures. ¶ I've gone out to the hive when I'm stressed or distracted. And the bees know. Beekeeping demands your full attention. You can't be thinking of other things. It's truly all-consuming.

HONEY, LEMON & ROSEMARY VINAIGRETTE

1 lemon, juiced

1 tbsp lemon zest
(from juiced lemon)

6 garlic cloves, roasted

1 tbsp grainy mustard

3 rosemary sprigs, stems
removed and leaves chopped

¼ cup honey (about 5 tbsp)

½ cup olive oil

salt and pepper to taste

Combine the lemon juice, lemon zest, roasted garlic, mustard, rosemary, and honey in a blender or food processor. Blend on high while slowly adding olive oil, until emulsified. Season with salt and pepper to taste.

To roast garlic, preheat your oven (or toaster oven) to 400°F. Peel and discard the papery outer layers of the garlic bulb. Leave skins intact on individual garlic cloves. Use a sharp knife to trim ¼-inch from top of cloves. Cover entire garlic head with aluminum foil, and place the garlic head on a baking sheet, trimmed side up. Bake for 30 to 40 minutes or until cloves are soft when pressed. Let cool, then squeeze roasted garlic out of skins.

Joaquim & Amor Conde

Farmers, Quinta Do Conde

An innovative, biodiverse organic farm offering harvest dinners & rural living courses.

Before moving to the County, I owned an automotive shop in Toronto. Business was good, but by the time I was twenty-eight, I weighed 210 pounds. I knew I needed to change my diet. ¶ I took an interest in gardening and started shopping at farmers' markets. That's where I met Vicki, of Vicki's Veggies. It was 9:30 a.m. and I was strolling through the market half-asleep. Out of nowhere, she shoved a carrot in my face and said, "You've gotta have this!" That fall, I came to one of her tomato tastings, and we moved here two years later. Vicki's been a big ambassador for the County. ¶ The farm started because we wanted to eat the best food possible. We're in the value-added business of farming. Because we're a small-acreage farm, we have to be creative. We can only raise three pigs to maturity on this farm without destroying the land. So we have to take the meat from those three pigs and turn it into the highest-value products possible. And that takes collaboration with other people. ¶ We're trying to rebuild this little farm and make it productive like it was, you know, maybe a hundred years ago. But of course, being out here, at some point you realize you need to pay the bills. So you've got to start producing a bit more. And our ten chickens no longer cut it. Now we have a hundred. We started with ten, and now we have twenty duck hens. We planted an orchard. We have ten acres, so our garden will probably grow to two acres. We're sort of arriving at our comfort level with the numbers of animals that we can sustainably maintain. ¶ We believe in agriculture that builds community instead of destroying it, like big agriculture does. It's so much better to work with and support the people around you. To me, food security is a bigger issue than just people who can't really access food because of their financial means. There's another component, which is the fact that we rely on a huge percentage of food imports. We actually have very few people who produce food here. There's a huge imbalance in production. We need those new farmers, young farmers, and that will increase our real food security. ¶ I also want to encourage people to make their own food. It's so much better, and it's a lot of fun. ¶ They say that a farm without animals is like a garden with no flowers. Animals are a huge component of developing a biodynamic farm system. If you don't have animals, you don't have manure and you need to bring fertilizer in from somewhere else. I'm always thinking about how to harvest as much as possible and not let anything go to waste. We have a duck pond, and one day we realized it's basically pre-fertilized water. It's another way we can capture as much as possible. ¶ We grow almost everything that grows in this climate. Potatoes, beans, peas. We have early brassicas, which are very big in my culture, Portuguese culture, like rapini and early kale. They're wonderful early-season greens. ¶ Our favourite part of the day is midday because we always stop, make lunch, drink wine, and spend an hour or two reviewing the day. We have a long, slow lunch and then go back to work till 9:00 p.m. To me, it makes it feel like it's worth it.

CHANFANA

This is one of those dishes that reconnects us to food. The kind of food that our grand-mothers would cook. The kind of food that left everyone feeling great, that made a hard day's work worth it. This is, to us, the true embodiment of Slow Food, comfort food, winter food, nose to tail. But above all, this is simply good food. Traditionally, it's made with older goat or sheep, depending on the region of Portugal. Makes enough for a good-sized party (but leftovers are even better the next day).

2 lbs leg meat, deboned and roughly cut in 2" cubes

2 lbs mixed neck and shoulder chops

3½ oz the best smoked bacon you can find, cut into strips

1 tbsp lard

1 tsp paprika

1 generous dash of olive oil

2 medium onions, cut thinly into rings

5 garlic cloves, crushed

5 whole dried cloves

1 bunch fresh parsley, stems removed and coarsely chopped (or about ½ cup)

1 bay leaf

salt and pepper to taste

4 cups red wine (full body/lots of tannins is best)

Combine all ingredients except wine and mix thoroughly in an ovenproof dish. Let sit for 1 hour.

Preheat oven to 400°F. Stir in wine to cover all the ingredients, and put into oven. After 1 hour, lower temperature to 350°F and cover with a lid or foil, cooking for about 3 to 4 hours more. Partway through cooking, remove the lid and add more wine if you feel it's needed. Adjust salt and pepper to taste, and continue cooking until tender.

Serve meat sprinkled with chopped parsley, simple boiled potatoes, and seasonal steamed leafy greens like rapini or turnip greens. There will be lots of sauce to soak the potatoes in. Wipe your plate clean with homemade sourdough bread. Pairs wonderfully with any full-bodied red wine.

Old goat is hard to find, and cooking time may vary, depending on the meats used. If using more tender cuts, the dish is ready when the meat is thoroughly tender and falls off the bone (usually about 2 to 3 hours total).

Jenifer Dean

General Manager/Cidermaker, The County Cider Company
An award-winning cider company producing quality hard ciders since 1995.

I'd say I have become a reluctant apple farmer. I joined County Cider in 2000 after I attended the first-ever Prince Edward County Winegrowers Association annual general meeting. There were only six members of PECWA at that time, and I was just there out of interest. One of the guest speakers was Mary Taylor, a professor from the new Wine Technology program at Loyalist College. I talked to her after the meeting, and Grant Howes, the grandfather of Ontario cidermaking and founder of The County Cider Company, happened to be standing there. He overheard our conversation and said, "Well, Jenifer, if you're interested in becoming a winemaker, you should come and work for me. I just planted a vineyard!" That was the year I turned forty. I had worked as a server and travel agent for over twenty years and needed to make a change. So as a single mom with two kids, I went back to school full-time for winemaking and started working for Grant at County Cider at the same time. ¶ Over the years, I became more involved with the entire business operation, overseeing not only wine- and cidermaking but also the retail store and the start-up of our restaurant. After Grant passed away in 2017, I also had to take on the added responsibility for the orchard. I like the idea of apple farming. But the reality is it's really, really hard. Knowing what to spray, when to spray, how much to spray—and then actually making it happen when you can't get the tractor out because it rained and the sprayer's too heavy to get through the wet ground. I've got great people who work with me, but I'm the one who has to figure out how to make sure we're going to have apples. ¶ I'm always surprised at harvest time by how many more apples we have than I thought we would. I'll walk through the orchard and think, "I don't see any apples in these trees," because they're really hard to see when they're small and they're green. ¶ I love how they change colours. Take the Northern Spy apple. As they grow, they're relatively pinky greeny, and the colours are streaky. In the last few days, because of the cold nights, they turn red, just like that. ¶ The best part of my job is being a mentor. I like working with other people, and teaching and assisting them to do their jobs. But that's also a challenge. Human resources has become ninety-five percent of what I do now. The other five percent is paperwork. ¶ I love living on the farm, walking out there every day. And the view—this morning, I was walking the dog out there when the sun was coming up, and I thought, "This isn't the worst place to live, is it?"

HARD CIDER CHEDDAR DIP

8 oz cream cheese

2 tsp Dijon mustard

2½ cups shredded extra-sharp cheddar cheese

¼ tsp Tabasco sauce

1 tsp Worcestershire sauce

¼–½ cup Waupoos or County Premium hard apple cider

salt and pepper to taste

Combine cream cheese, mustard, cheddar, Tabasco, and Worcestershire sauce in a heavy-bottomed pan.

Cook on low heat for about 15 to 20 minutes, stirring occasionally, until cheese is melted and mixture is smooth.

Add cider gradually while stirring, until the thickness of the dip is to your liking. Season with salt and pepper.

Serve dip warm with lightly toasted bread chunks and apple slices.

Neil Dowson

Chef, Midtown Brewing Company
Neil originally hails from Coventry, England & is a Chopped Canada winner.

I moved to Canada nine years ago, after my daughter was born. We landed in Prince Edward County by accident. We were going to move to Niagara because I had a friend who was a chef at a winery there. But an acquaintance suggested the County, so I sent out my resumé on a whim, and that was that. We turned up one weekend waiting for our stuff to arrive from England in a big container. We knew from our first week that this is where we wanted to live. ¶ When I was training to be a chef in England, I got a job at an award-winning pub in the Midlands. The Savoy Hotel used to do a road show, and luckily they spent three days at my school. At the end of it, I was selected to move to London to work at the Savoy. ¶ It was one of the top five hotels in the world, with 120 chefs in the kitchen. My first six months were spent preparing vegetables. That's it. Then I spent six months working in the fish department. I'd show up and there'd be 2,000 scallops in shells, fifty salmon, an enormous room full of fish. And then six months preparing the meat, and so on. And then you're allowed in the kitchen to cook after two years. That's almost like your apprenticeship. And then you're allowed onto the stove to actually cook. I left after six years, as a sous-chef. It was the best place I could have gone to cook. ¶ I ended up working as the executive chef at a hotel group. Whenever they'd open a new hotel, I'd set up the kitchen, stay for a year, and then head to another one. The County is the first place where we decided we're not leaving, where we can make actual friends. ¶ I started at the Waring House; it was the only place that offered me full-time. And then Kimberly called me from East & Main, and so I decided to try something else. But I only stayed there for a summer, because the Agrarian was just moving from a coffee shop to wanting to be a restaurant. So that was great timing. ¶ I was at the Agrarian for two years. It was a nice place. Good, tiny kitchen. And then I left Agrarian for County Road Beer, for time, quality of life. They closed at 5:00 p.m. every day, so I didn't have to miss time with my kids. ¶ I spent two years at County Road. I think we had a really, really good thing—it was something very cool. But unfortunately, the brewery closed, and it was time to move on again. Luckily, the timing was right, as Midtown was looking for a chef. ¶ Midtown is moulded in a very British style. I've always cooked whatever I want to cook here, because I know British food better than anyone else. Sixty percent of our menu is what the average person wants to eat, and for the other forty percent I do something a little bit different. ¶ I'm a very different chef than I was ten or fifteen years ago. I used to work in Michelin-star restaurants, but I have a great work-life balance at Midtown. I get to spend time with my family instead of working fifteen-hour days in the kitchen. And I have complete freedom to cook whatever I want. That's a great chef's life.

IRISH STOUT
4.2% ABV
4 PK $14
ESB
5.4% ABV
6 PAK $21
COUNTY KOLSCH
473ml CANS
TAKE OUT $3.50
TAKE OUT $3.50
PLEASE PAY FOR CANS @MAIN BAR! THX. MBC
MIDTOWN BREWING CO
Ontario

BEEF & ALE PIE

Filling

2 lbs boneless stewing beef (diced into 1" pieces)

2 tbsp all-purpose flour

1 tbsp salt

1 large onion, diced

2 cups dark ale or stout

2 cups beef broth

2 tbsp Worcestershire sauce

2 tbsp tomato paste

2 sprigs thyme

2 bay leaves

Pastry

2¼ cups all-purpose flour

1 cup hard butter, cut into ½" cubes

⅜ cups cold water

¼ tsp salt

1 egg, beaten

To prepare the filling, begin by mixing flour and salt in a small bowl. Roll the diced beef in the mix, shaking off any excess flour.

Sear the beef in an ovenproof pot in small batches in a little oil until dark brown and seared.

Add onions and cook for 3 minutes, then deglaze with the beer. Cook for 3 minutes to remove all beef flavour from the pan by scraping the bottom of the pot.

Add beef broth, Worcestershire sauce, tomato paste, thyme, bay leaves. Cover with a lid and cook at 300°F in the oven for approximately 2 hours, or until the beef is tender.

For the pastry top, place flour and salt in food processor. Pulse in the hard butter until mixture resembles a bread-crumb consistency. Place mixture in a bowl and slowly add the cold water until it forms a dough. Cover with plastic wrap and refrigerate for 1 hour.

Drain excess sauce from beef; reserve. Place the beef mix (and enough sauce to moisten) into a medium-sized ovenproof dish.

Roll out pastry dough to approximate ¼-inch thickness. Place over dish, brush with the egg, and cook at 300°F for approximately 1 hour.

Serve with creamed potatoes and your favourite vegetables, with the reserved sauce alongside.

Vicki Emlaw

Farmer, Vicki's Veggies

A small farm best known for its 100+ varieties of heirloom tomatoes & being a local cultural hub.

I'm an eighth-generation South Marysburgher. After high school, I went to Carlton University for business, and then geography, and then did my own in-depth geographical study. I spent the next twelve years travelling around the world, and would come home for the summer and work in restaurants around the County. ¶ None of my friends lived here anymore, so I gardened all day. I knew very little about gardening. I was twenty-five and I had no idea what basil was. I bought leek seedlings from Diane Walker—I had never eaten a leek before. ¶ I started working at the Waupoos Pub, and the owner, Chris DaSilva, bought everything I grew to make up her menu each day for lunch and dinner. At first, I basically took over my mom's garden. In 2000, when I moved to Morrison Point Road, my dad helped me plow my original field. And that was how I started. ¶ In 2016, I took a break from farming and signed up for a yoga teacher training course in the Bahamas. It was an intensive month: no alcohol, no meat, no coffee, up at 6:00 a.m. every day—it sounded like a great vacation to me. ¶ When I arrived, they gave me a karma yoga job. On my application, I'd written that I'd been a gardener for twenty years, and I wanted to work in the kitchen so I could learn to make vegetarian food. But they needed me in the garden; they needed someone who knew how to dig a hole, plant flowers, and make things look beautiful. My motto used to be "If you can't eat it, don't grow it." But what's not to love about gardening in the Bahamas, with all of those beautiful tropical plants? There were ten different varieties of hibiscus alone. ¶ While I was at the ashram, I spent the whole time in the garden in my bare feet, really grounding myself and reconnecting to the earth. Strangers who were there for a day were coming up to me and saying, "You look like you belong there in the garden." I learned that the connection I have with the earth is a gift, that I'm really at home in the garden, and capable of creating life. ¶ And so when I came back home, that's when I decided I needed to keep saving seeds from the heirloom tomatoes I'd collected over the past sixteen years. Some of these heirloom tomatoes are hundreds of years old. I've found and collected some extremely rare heirloom tomatoes and I will do all I can to keep them alive and not let them become extinct—I feel responsible for them. They're like my children. I feel like they've chosen me. ¶ There are about 260 different varieties of tomatoes in my greenhouse right now. I plant the number of seeds I think I need, plus a little bit extra for all the other heirloom tomato superfans out there like me. I feel like I'm making magic happen. From these tiny little seeds, wondrous plants grow, produce nourishing fruit, create beauty, and taste great. And to me, that's really exciting.

PANZANELLA

Croutons

½ large baguette,
cut into large chunks

salt and pepper to taste

fresh thyme and rosemary to taste

Salad

6–8 lbs heirloom tomatoes,
cut into chunks

1 red onion, cut into
slivered wedges

¼–½ lb mozzarella,
cut into cubes

1 handful fresh basil,
coarsely chopped

12 pitted olives (optional)

1 cup each cucumber and/or
pepper chunks (optional)

Dressing

⅔ cup olive oil

1½ tbsp balsamic vinegar

¼ cup red wine vinegar

1 tbsp Dijon mustard

2 tbsp honey

2 garlic cloves

1 handful fresh basil

salt and pepper to taste

> Using fresh mozzarella cheese
> makes this great salad even
> better.

To prepare the croutons, in a large bowl, toss baguette chunks together with enough olive oil to lightly coat, adding salt, pepper, thyme, and rosemary.

Spread in an even layer onto a large baking sheet.

Bake at 350°F for about 25 to 30 minutes, or until evenly toasted, stirring occasionally.

To prepare the salad, toss all ingredients together.

To prepare the dressing, combine all ingredients in food processor and blend.

Just before serving, add dressing to salad, then toss with giant croutons.

Jenna Empey

Head Grower/Fermenter, Pyramid Ferments
Handcrafted, raw, live & fermented sauerkraut, kimchi & kombucha.

I had a scholarship to attend university in British Columbia but I dropped out after one semester because there was something pulling me to work with my hands. ¶ I moved to Halifax, even though I only knew a single person in the entire province. That's where I met Alex (Alex Currie, the other half of Pyramid Ferments). We started a band the week we met. But I missed my connection to food, missed the farm, the garden. ¶ I moved back to the County at the end of 2011 and decided to stay. I said, "Hey, Alex, do you want to live in an unheated trailer and work really hard in the middle of nowhere?" And he answered, "Absolutely." ¶ The first year, we grew a few rows of cabbage and used them in one go. And I thought, "What are we going to do?" ¶ We hooked up with Hagerman Farms. Fiddlehead Farm has grown so much for us. We found lots of farmers and local producers who are happy to grow with us. It's been amazing. ¶ Cabbage is not a sexy vegetable. No one wants to grow it. It takes a long growing season. It's huge. It's delicious though. ¶ We don't follow recipes. We have general recipe guidelines but we taste our way through it. Fermenting is like cooking—are you the cook who follows the recipe or the cook who just figures it out? ¶ Even though we're in major chain grocery stores, we still maintain an agricultural connection. We still grow a lot of the weirder herbs ourselves. We do wild crafting and foraging for kombucha flavours and special-batch kimchis. We keep things superlocal, superfresh, and focus on really intriguing flavours. I'll take whatever I can find in the field, in the garden, in the woods and turn it into a new flavour that no one's ever tried before. ¶ Fermenting is a belief in the unseen. It's magic. There's so much going on in each barrel, each vessel that you can't see. But you have to anticipate and guide the results. ¶ The whole point of Pyramid Ferments is to make food that really helps people. It's amazing to think that you can provide that for somebody, that they'll put their trust in you to help their body function in a different way.

DILL & GARLIC SAUERKRAUT

1 head green cabbage
(approximately 10 cups),
outer leaves discarded

1¼ tsp finely ground sea salt or
pink Himalayan salt

1½ tbsp garlic, finely chopped

2 tbsp chopped fresh dill

> Make sure your salt is not coarsely ground and has no added iodine or running agents, as this will affect the fermentation. To sterilize jar and lids, clean well, rinse, and dip into boiling hot water.

Quarter the cabbage lengthwise, removing the core. Finely slice the cabbage into long, thin strips approximately 5 inches long and ⅛-inch wide. Place the slices into a large, sturdy metal or plastic mixing bowl. Add the salt, garlic, and dill.

Mix, massage, and squeeze the cabbage with your hands until well mixed and the cabbage begins to let out some of its juices, approximately 8 to 10 minutes. Be sure not to undermix or overmix, or pound into mush, as it will not ferment properly.

Pack the mixed ingredients into a sterilized 1 L glass canning jar. Pack mixture down until the brine rises over the top layer of cabbage. Fill up to the jar's shoulders; do not fill to the very top.

Wipe down the neck and rim of the jar and apply either a tight-fitting #13 drilled rubber stopper with an airlock (available at winemaking supply stores) or a baggie filled with salted water to create a water weight on the surface of the sauerkraut. Secure it with an elastic band and cover with a dishtowel or piece of fabric. Place jar on a dish in case it overflows.

Every few days, push the sauerkraut down with the back of a fork until the brine rises up over the cabbage, fermenting in room temperature of 64°F to 69°F, for 7 to 14 days. Sample the sauerkraut until it reaches your desired sourness. Once fermented, cover with a plastic jar lid and refrigerate. For optimum flavour, eat your refrigerated sauerkraut within 4 months.

Andreas Feller

Chef, Blumen Garden Bistro

At Blumen, Andy serves up seasonally inspired signature bistro meals.

I was born in Switzerland and did my cooking apprenticeship there, then spent ten years in Venezuela. The smartest thing for me to do would have been to go home to Switzerland and take over my dad's business. He was an interior designer and salesman and architect. Instead, I moved to Ottawa, where I became a chef. ¶ I worked at the Glue Pot Pub. Lots of government workers came in, and I worked the day shift. Then, after a stint at a breakfast joint in Gatineau, I started at e18hteen, one of the first high-end places in Ottawa. Just a fabulous place. I hadn't cooked yet in any establishment in a proper kitchen for twelve years. And it was like, here's my chance, I've got my foot in, now I have to walk the talk. So I worked hard and became sous-chef and that's when I said, "Okay, now this is it." ¶ I was well-trained in French cooking and all this classic stuff. But this was my first exposure to fusion, the more modern style of fine dining. ¶ Then, after trying to make a couple of moves, I became so disenchanted with working in a kitchen that I decided I was never going to cook again. I went to a job counsellor and they made me do a 300-question quiz. And the results said that I should be a chef. So my then-wife asked me, "Why don't we try something ourselves?" ¶ We started looking for an inn with a dining room. We looked everywhere, from the East Coast all the way to Alberta. When the realtor first brought us to the building Blumen is in now, I remember walking in and thinking it was so wrong. There were curtains everywhere to cover stains on the walls. The yard was overgrown. The house had been abandoned for years. But my wife, she saw the potential. ¶ We bought the place at a bargain price and did all the renovations ourselves. One evening in June, I was laying the floor for the restaurant. And I looked across the street and saw an ocean of fireflies. I took a break, walked across the road, and sat down and gazed at the fireflies. It was the most beautiful thing. ¶ A year later we opened. It was July 21, a Sunday evening. It rained so hard that we lost power. Some of the food went inexplicably bad, and we had to rush out to replace it. Things were going so horribly that I started crying. But we had twenty-four people in the book that night. And we did twenty-four people the next night, and twenty-seven the third night. It was amazing. ¶ The first evening we opened, after everybody went home, I locked up and I just stood there, stunned. It was hard to believe it had actually happened. There were so many moments when I didn't think we'd make it. We were really just a couple of people who knew how to cook and decided to wing the rest. And it worked.

QUICHE LORRAINE

Butter Shell

2 cups flour

1 tsp salt

1 pinch pepper

1 cup cold butter, cut into pieces

¼ cup ice water

dry beans (for pre-baking)

Quiche Lorraine Filling

1 tbsp cooking oil

1¾ cup onion, sliced

2 cups double-smoked bacon, sliced into pieces, but not too fine; slab bacon is best

1½ cups Gruyère cheese, finely grated

¾ cup milk

2 cups 5% cream

8 eggs

2 tbsp flour

¼ tsp nutmeg

salt and pepper to taste

> To help reduce baking time, warm the egg mixture in a double boiler until just beginning to thicken, before transferring to the pre-baked pastry shell.

To prepare butter shell, add flour to stand mixer with paddle, or to a food processor. Add butter, salt, and pepper, and mix till incorporated. Or use a pastry cutter to mix the ingredients by hand. Bring the mixture to point where the butter is pea-sized and the flour is in pellets. Add just enough water to bring the dough together; it's okay if there are dry parts. Gently patty it together while trying not to overwork it. Let rest 1 to 8 hours.

Oil a 10-inch springform pan. Dust dough with flour and roll it out to about 16-inch round. Roll the dough up on the pin and gently unfold over the springform pan. Press into corners using a piece of excess dough (so dough doesn't rip). Leave some hanging over the edge. Let rest 30 minutes in fridge.

Fork the bottom. Heat oven to 350°F. Set parchment paper over dough and fill with dried beans. Pre-bake for 30 minutes or until dough is lightly brown, then remove beans and bake another 15 minutes.

To prepare filling, add oil to pan and cook onions while covered for about 10 minutes, till soft, taking care not to brown them too much. Set onions aside. In the same pan, cook bacon over medium-low heat for about 10 minutes or until fat is released and the meat is crisp and browned; let cool. Grate the Gruyère using the fine side of your grater. Combine onions, bacon, Gruyère, milk, cream, eggs, and flour in a large bowl. Using a wooden spoon, stir well. Add nutmeg, salt, and pepper. Transfer mixture to the pre-baked butter shell.

Bake at 350°F for 60 to 90 minutes, starting to check after 60 minutes; keep checking till egg is set. Let cool in pan. Chill overnight before cutting. To serve, reheat for 15 to 20 minutes. Serve with salad of choice.

Mike Fountoukis

Chef, Gus's Family Restaurant
A classic diner & Picton Main Street fixture.

I stick to tried-and-true. We're not the type of place to switch up the menus. You can't really do that in a diner. This is really country-style food, like hot sandwiches. But I use local produce when it's in season. ¶ Gus's has been here for thirty years. We were the Burger Palace first, and then we turned into Gus's. My mom and dad started the place. My dad worked in the restaurant business, and they decided to open a place on their own. It was hard because my dad worked seven days a week all his life. He only took Christmas off. And never ate dinner at home. But other than that, I thought it was a cool job. ¶ My parents had to work to establish the business. Now that it's more established, I get to spend a lot more time with my kids. You know, it's a little different now than it was back then when I was growing up. ¶ My dad, Gus, passed away when he was sixty-four. He kept everything, all his recipes, everything in his head. He never wrote anything down. His motto was "If you don't pay attention, you'll never learn." So he never taught you. You just watched. Even down to the basics, like cutting tomatoes, because he might get two more slices out of that tomato than I would. ¶ My mom still works in the afternoons, because I open. I go home for two hours and then I come back and close every night. ¶ I thought about going into high-end cooking. That was my dream. But then I fell in love with this style, because it's high-paced. And I'm a high-paced guy. It's a little different now that I own the restaurant. Obviously, there's more stress. But I still love it. ¶ Things have changed. New Year's used to be our biggest day, and then it became Mother's Day, and now it's Father's Day. In general, it seems like people want more high-end meals. But that's not what we do. My favourite things to cook are fish. Liver. ¶ I'm gonna keep cooking as long as I can, like my dad.

OF MAKING
A FEW MORE.

HAPPY HOLIDAYS

I can only please
one person per day.

Today is not your day.

Tomorrow doesn't
look good, either.

Prices Subject
To Change...
According to customer's
ATTITUDE

BUNN
BUNN

IF YOU DON'T
WORK HERE
I DON'T WANT
YOU BEHIND
THIS COUNTER

Why is there never
time to do it right,
but there is always
time to do it

STRIKE

Mike

BAKLAVA

⅔ cup chopped walnuts

⅔ cup chopped almonds

⅔ cup chopped pistachios

¼ cup + 1 tbsp sugar

1 tsp cinnamon

½ box (454 g) phyllo sheets

1 stick butter, melted, for brushing

Syrup

1 cup water

¼ cup + 1 tbsp sugar

½ cup Greek honey

¼ tsp vanilla

1 large piece lemon rind

1 tbsp lemon juice

In pot, combine all ingredients for syrup. Bring to a boil and simmer for 10 minutes. Remove from heat and let cool at room temperature. Remove lemon rind.

Preheat oven to 350°F.

In a large mixing bowl, combine all nuts, sugar, and cinnamon.

Use a sharp knife (or pizza wheel) to cut 10 sheets of phyllo to fit an 8-inch square baking pan. Keep phyllo covered with a damp kitchen towel while assembling, to prevent from drying out.

Lightly grease pan with a little melted butter. Add one sheet phyllo and brush with butter. Repeat 5 times. Sprinkle half the nut mixture evenly over phyllo. Add 2 more phyllo sheets; brush with butter between sheets. Add rest of nut mixture. Top with 3 phyllo sheets.

Use a sharp knife with a very thin blade to score baklava into diamond-shaped pieces, cutting through all phyllo layers. Place pan in oven and cook for 30 minutes. Remove and pour cooled syrup evenly over hot baklava. Let cool before serving, dusted with additional cinnamon.

Ruth Gangbar

Food Stylist; Chef, Ruth's Canteen
Food photography stylist & recipe editor, with a side of community-driven provisioner.

My first job was in a fish market, and I can still fillet a fish on a rock in the dark—almost. I didn't know very much about fish or seafood, and there was a Help Wanted sign in this incredible Toronto fish shop at Yonge and Summerhill. The woman who ran it was the most interesting character; she was a wedding dress designer, and her father owned the Henry H. Misner fish plant in Port Dover, which was a big commercial fishery that caught a lot of perch and smelt. And I needed a job. So I tripped in there and got swept into a training program and ended up co-managing some other fish markets in the early eighties. ¶ I also worked as a baker at the Queen Mother Café, and for a whole bunch of small commercial bakeries. ¶ I did food styling for the LCBO's *Food and Drink* magazine for over twelve years, and it was a privilege. I really enjoyed working with some of the best food stylists, prop stylists, photographers, and art directors who brought their best game. ¶ I've got an eye for composition—the food and the plating. It's intuition. I really like things that aren't symmetrical—that's where the crumbs land. Let that ooze happen. There are technical exercises and lots of tricks with food styling, but for me it can be incredibly organic. I've learned that after twenty-five years of food styling. ¶ Instagram and iPhones have really enabled people to feel quite confident that the work they're able to do anoints them with this level of qualification. And I think it's wonderful to be creative and experimental, but you can't blow those images up to make banners for farm stands. ¶ I've always loved the farm stands here. For one thing, they've made me kind of a hero. I'll show up to photo shoots in Toronto with gorgeous sweet potatoes, and they photograph beautifully, and I can say where the food came from, and talk about these people's lives. ¶ In 1994, I bought a dilapidated "fisherman's delight" cabin here in the County. It was right on the water and in a beautiful spot, very secluded. It just had a great vibe. There's a United Empire Loyalists cemetery right beside it. ¶ I've been working as a food stylist in Toronto and oscillating back and forth between the city and the County for so many years. I want to try a simpler approach, to be a little more self-sufficient and try to grow more food. I like eating and feeding, and also learning from a lot of people out here who have a great deal of knowledge. I'm kind of a sponge. So I'm reinventing myself here with more commitment to the community at large. ¶ Now I've started holding food pop-ups as Ruth's Canteen, which is incredibly satisfying.

CARROT & TRIPLE-CHOCOLATE CUPCAKES

Cupcakes

½ cup unsalted butter,
room temperature

1 cup light brown sugar (reserve
1 tbsp for beating egg whites)

3 eggs, separated

2 tsp vanilla

½ tsp almond extract

1 cup coarsely grated carrots
(about 3 medium carrots)

1½ cups all-purpose flour

½ cup cocoa powder

2½ tsp ground cinnamon

½ tsp freshly grated nutmeg

1 tsp baking soda

½ tsp baking powder

1 cup buttermilk

⅓ cup semi-sweet chocolate chips

Icing

½ cup unsalted butter,
softened to room temperature

1 cup icing sugar

⅔ cup cocoa

1 tsp vanilla extract

¼ cup buttermilk

Decoration

½ package (227 g) marzipan

orange food colouring
(8 drops red, 10–16 drops yellow)

Using a hand mixer, beat together the butter and brown sugar until fluffy. Add the egg yolks, vanilla, and almond extract, beating again until fluffy. Stir in grated carrots. Set aside.

In large bowl, sift together the flour, cocoa powder, cinnamon, nutmeg, baking soda, and baking powder.

Combine one third of the flour mixture into the butter mixture, alternating with half the buttermilk. Repeat, beginning and ending with the flour. Fold in the chocolate chips to combine evenly. Beat remaining eggs whites with a hand mixer until frothy. Add reserved 1 tablespoon sugar, continuing to beat until stiff. Gently fold into the batter until just blended. Divide batter into the paper-lined muffin tins. Bake in 375°F oven for about 25 minutes, or until springy to the touch. Cool completely on a baking rack.

For icing, combine butter, icing sugar, and cocoa using an electric mixer (or food processor fitted with a steel blade) for 1 minute or until fluffy and smooth. Add vanilla and buttermilk, and combine until smooth.

For marzipan carrots, knead the marzipan to soften, while blending with orange food colouring until evenly combined. Form into 12 small carrot shapes. (If desired, roll the edge of a small knife around the carrots, making light indentations.) Make a small hole in the top of each carrot with a toothpick and press a fresh carrot leaf into the hole.

Decorate cooled cupcakes with chocolate icing and top each with a marzipan carrot.

Enid Grace

Owner, Enid Grace Culinary

Dedicated to food, recipes, living well, travel & entrepreneurship.

I'm from Rednersville, Ontario. I grew up cooking with my mother and grandmother. I can trace my interest in Italy back to the third grade. We did a world study where we were each assigned countries, and I got Italy. ¶ I took my first trip to Europe when I was fifteen. I had a very strong feeling right away that I was destined to be there. ¶ I became superinterested in cookbooks and I collected a library. I read them like novels, and studied and studied. And then, as it became easier to do even more research with the internet, I would go full bore into a recipe's history, how it had changed over the years. ¶ After taking on a few marketing jobs, I went back to Italy and got involved with Slow Food by going to the actual birthplace of the movement. I travelled around and stayed with families for three to six months and learned whatever it was they were doing. I had this cheeky thing of flirting with guys so I could get to their mothers and grandmothers. It was a sneaky way to get into their kitchens and get their grandmothers to show me how to make pasta. ¶ There are classic schools and culinary training, but the backbone of all of it is what you learn in your grandmother's kitchen and then trying it on your own. I took that very much to heart. I had no interest in culinary school, and I decided I could teach myself over long stretches of time, through trial and error and study. I pored over 200-year-old recipes and tried to figure out the alchemy of why certain recipes have stood the test of time and why they're so beloved all over the world. ¶ It became pretty clear that Prince Edward County was not the Prince Edward County of my childhood, that there was opportunity here. So for one full summer, I set up an international food stand that featured food from a different country I'd either lived in, travelled to, or was interested in. I folded that into the café, which I really wanted to be a classic northern Italian café. But I had to be realistic that North Americans don't eat or recognize mornings the same way Italians, French, Spaniards do. So I had to make some concessions. I gave everyone what I knew they wanted. ¶ I want to stretch, and I want the community to be able to stretch and have more opportunities to experience different things. Under the umbrella of Enid Grace Culinary, I'm dropping the short order and providing an even more heightened Italian coffee and pastry bar experience with Piccolina, the little café. Enid's Table is the dining part, and then the teaching kitchen in the back. So it's kind of a replication of places I saw in Italy.

SPINACH & RICOTTA GNUDI WITH HERB BUTTER SAUCE

Gnudi

250 g drained whole milk
fresh ricotta

1 lb fresh spinach (about 10 cups)

25 g freshly grated
Parmigiano Reggiano

1 large fresh egg (lightly beaten)

1 tbsp lemon zest
(from 1 medium lemon)

pinch salt

1 tbsp all-purpose flour,
plus more for dusting

Sauce

40 g unsalted butter

5–6 fresh sage leaves

2 sprigs fresh thyme

salt to taste

To Serve

2–3 tbsp Parmigiano Reggiano,
freshly grated

nutmeg, freshly grated, to taste

The ricotta and spinach need to be as dry as possible to ensure that the delicate gnudi don't fall apart when simmering.

Line a mesh sieve with cheesecloth and set over a bowl. Place ricotta in sieve and allow to drain for 1 to 2 hours. Weigh out 250 grams after the liquid has drained away. Set aside.

Add the fresh spinach to a large sauté pan with a few splashes of hot water to help wilt the greens. Cover with a lid and cook for 3 to 5 minutes, until all the spinach is wilted. Drain the spinach in a sieve, pressing down to extract as much liquid as possible. Roughly chop into tiny pieces (weigh the spinach after this step to ensure you have at least 300 grams of cooked chopped spinach). Set aside in a medium bowl.

In the same bowl with the spinach, mix the ricotta, Parmigiano Reggiano, beaten egg, lemon zest, salt, and 1 tablespoon of flour (if needed to absorb any excess moisture). Make sure everything is incorporated but don't overwork the mixture; you want the gnudi to be light.

Place additional flour in a dish. Roll pieces of the mixture in between your palms to create small balls of gnudi, about 20 to 25 grams each. Gently roll each one in the bowl of flour to lightly coat them. Place the dusted balls onto a dry, clean board with space between them. Allow to rest while you continue shaping the remaining mixture.

Heat a large skillet on low heat. Gently melt the butter. Add sage leaves and thyme sprigs. Keep warm while you cook the gnudi.

Fill a large pot with salted water and bring to a gentle simmer. Slowly lower in the gnudi and let them gently cook for about 5 minutes or until they float to the top. (Depending on the size of your pot, you may need to cook them in 2 batches as to not overcrowd. You don't want them pressed up against each other in the hot water.) Remove with a slotted spoon and gently lay them in the warm butter.

Gently swirl the gnudi in the butter to coat. Plate the gnudi, adding a few spoonfuls of the herb butter over top (add the sage leaves and any thyme leaves that have fallen off the sprig to the plate as well). Finish with a generous rain of fresh Parmigiano Reggiano over top and a few gratings of fresh nutmeg. There will be no leftovers!

Leah Marshall Hannon

Chef, Stella's Eatery

Named after Leah's great-grandmother, Stella's features local, fresh, foraged, seasonal food.

I was looking on Kijiji for leases, and the Milford Bistro came up. That's what brought me here. And then it fell through. I got a call from Sand and Pearl, and they offered me the chef position to open that place up, so I did that for a summer. And then I wanted to open my own place. ¶ I named the restaurant after my great-grandma, Stella. It's also one of my middle names. I wanted it to be an homage to the thankless job of being a matriarch, and finding comfort in that. My dad's Ojibwe, and my introduction to Indigenous cooking came from my aunt Florence. She told me a lot about Stella, who died from cancer when my dad was young. Stella cooked on this amazing woodstove. We'd go there every summer, and I'd learn about her pantry and what she used to cook through her recipes, about the traplines and what to cook in the winter when things were scarce. It was really eye-opening for me at a young age to learn to rationalize what to cook—that not everything came from a grocery store. ¶ I got my love of cooking from my family, especially my mom. My mom and my aunt catered for movie sets in Toronto. I remember we always ate leftovers, and it was amazing. My mom put my brother and me in a school called First Nations School of Toronto. It was for native First Nations kids, and we went there for two years and we'd have powwows and potlucks. I learned a lot from potlucks, like corn soup and bannock. Stewed goose. Wild rice. Different ways of cooking. ¶ Originally, I wanted to be a butcher. I worked at one place in Parry Sound, and the cook would never make a staff meal. I was like, sweet, I get to go in the kitchen and make it myself. So I'd pretend to be a chef and I'd be behind the line cooking myself a meal. And that's when I realized I really like cooking. ¶ I learned a lot when I worked at Delux. It was a little French bistro on Ossington in Toronto. We'd do 160 covers a night and bounce back and do it all again the next night. I'd never worked in an environment like that. But everyone was just lovely and took care of one another. I started as a chef de partie, as a cook and worked my way up the ranks. ¶ The initial idea for Stella's was to be a restaurant that was open from 9:00 a.m. to 9:00 p.m., which is insane. I learned that pretty quickly. I mean, you can only have four pots on our one stove at any given point. ¶ I want there to be more First Nations influence to my style of food. It's there, it's just not at the forefront, but I'm working on it. Now I focus on whatever the farmers give me. I check in with them weekly to see what's coming up, then set my menus and cook.

PICKEREL CAKES WITH FANCY TARTAR SAUCE & FENNEL SLAW

Pickerel Cakes

8 medium Yukon Gold potatoes

1 fillet fresh pickerel, skin on (about 6 oz)

1 tbsp sunflower oil

1 tbsp butter or oil

2 leeks, sliced

¼ cup chopped dill

2 tbsp chopped thyme

1 lemon, zested

salt to taste

2 whole eggs

2 tbsp water

3 cups bread crumbs

2 cups all-purpose flour

Fancy Tartar

1 cup mayonnaise

1 lemon, juiced

¼ cup chopped dill pickle

¼ cup chopped sweet pickle

2 tbsp minced shallot

2 tbsp grainy mustard

¼ cup chopped parsley

1 tbsp chopped thyme

a few dashes of your favourite hot sauce

salt and pepper to your liking

Crunchy Fennel Slaw

1 head fennel, trimmed and halved through base

1 Granny Smith apple

1 tsp lemon juice

1 tsp apple cider vinegar

1 tbsp Dijon mustard

1 tbsp sunflower oil

1 tbsp honey or cane sugar

For the pickerel cakes, boil Yukon Gold potatoes with the skins on until cooked through. Strain and set aside to cool. Preheat oven to 350°F. On a parchment-lined baking tray, lay the side of pickerel skin-side down. Season minimally with sunflower oil and salt. Cook fish for 20 minutes until flaky. Set aside to cool. In a saucepan, on medium heat, heat 2 tablespoons of butter or oil. Add chopped leeks. Season with salt to taste. Sweat down the leeks until cooked through. Add to large mixing bowl to cool. Once potatoes are cool (peel or don't peel, totally up to you), crumble them with your hands into the large mixing bowl with the cooked leeks. Check the cooked and cooled pickerel fillet for bones. Once all remaining bones are removed, flake fish apart using a fork. Again, skin on or off is up to your personal preference. Add flaked pickerel to the large mixing bowl. Chop and add herbs and zest to the pickerel cake mixture. Season with salt to your liking. Mix everything together until relatively smooth and incorporated. I personally like a bit of chunk and texture. Cover mixture and put in fridge while prepping the other elements.

For the fancy tartar, measure mayonnaise into a bowl. Mince pickles and shallot, and add to bowl. Chop herbs and add to bowl. Juice the zested lemon and add that too. Add mustard and hot sauce. Mix until smooth and incorporated.

For the fennel slaw, shave fennel thinly; if you have a mandoline slicer, now is the time to use it. This is the garnish for the cakes, so let's make it look pretty. If you don't have a mandoline, focus on slicing the fennel very thinly. I usually shave from where the stems and fronds of fennel are removed, to the base of the bulb. If doing this by hand, work with the flat side of the fennel facing down. Julienne the apple into fine matchstick pieces. In a medium-sized bowl, mix together lemon juice, apple cider vinegar, Dijon, oil, and sugar. Add fennel and apple; toss lightly.

To prepare the breading station, gather 3 medium-sized bowls. Add 2 eggs to the first; whisk eggs, then whisk in 2 tablespoons of water. Add flour to a second bowl and bread crumbs to the last.

Remove pickerel mixture from fridge and roll mixture into about ten 2-inch balls. Bread each ball by rolling it through the flour, then rolling it through the egg wash mixture, and finish by rolling it through the bread crumbs, making sure each cake is well coated. You can repeat this process if you want the cakes extra crispy.

Warm a medium-sized heavy skillet on medium heat, and add enough vegetable oil or butter (or a bit of both) to about an inch depth of oil in skillet. Fry the battered cakes until golden brown on both sides, turning carefully with two spatulas.

Once all of your cakes are browned and crispy and ready to be served, place on your favourite large serving platter. Add a healthy dollop of tartar to each cake and finish with a tight twirl of crunchy fennel slaw. Optional: Serve with a scallion garnish or a dusting of seaweed flakes. Somewhat labour intensive, but the end result is magical. Enjoy!

Jared Hartley

Chef, Hartleys Tavern

Hartleys Tavern is the culmination of Jim, Janine & Jared Hartley's passion for food.

I was born into the restaurant business, quite literally. My parents were scheduled to open their first restaurant in New York on October 3. My mom went into labour at 10:00 a.m., as she was running around town picking out light fixtures and artwork for the restaurant. She finally went to the hospital, and my dad left the restaurant to go with her. Everyone at the restaurant opening followed him and ended up at the hospital. It was literally a party when I was born. ¶ I grew up in that restaurant. And I've always enjoyed not just cooking, but restaurants in general. They're quite addictive. I love cooking immensely, but restaurants are what I really love, the whole scope of it. I even love the specifics of service. ¶ I've never done anything other than working in restaurants. When I went to high school, I did the Iron Chef program because I always wanted to be in the restaurant business. My parents insisted, "No, go get a real job." But I knew what I wanted. ¶ My parents managed the restaurant at Waupoos Estate Winery, and I worked there with Chef Lili Sullivan—I did a co-op with her husband, Chef Mike Sullivan, at the Merrill Inn too. They've been good mentors to me. I chose to go to Stratford Chefs School on multiple chefs' recommendations, including Mike's. ¶ I went to chef school right after high school and then opened Hartleys Tavern immediately after. I was nineteen. The first three days, I must have worked almost sixty hours. It was just me and one other person in the kitchen when we opened. I was washing dishes until five or six o'clock in the morning. ¶ I find managing is the hardest part of the job, hands down. There's no easy way to learn it—it's just about building relationships with people and understanding what each specific person needs. ¶ My favourite day in the County is when the onions come out. I drive by five or six farms on my way to work, and I get so excited to explore the stands to see what's in season and which vegetables look especially great. ¶ The only thing I can't really get in the County is fry potatoes. And it's just something that's not going to change, because russet potatoes just don't get big enough here. And it's unfortunate, but nobody likes small, shitty fries. ¶ I enjoy making my own bread. It's a labour of love, and it takes a lot of work. But when I pull a loaf of bread out of the oven, sometimes I can't help but walk around the restaurant with it, like it's a big fish I just caught. ¶ I love just after service ends on a busy day, chit spike full to the brim. The last couple of tables are finishing up. And you think back on the evening and realize how well your entire crew did. But my favourite part of the workday is when my mom comes into work.

MOUSSE DE FOIE

500 g trimmed duck, chicken, or rabbit livers

200 g room-temperature butter

200 g chilled rendered duck fat

500 ml 35% cream

6 eggs

30 ml brandy

15 g salt

3 g white pepper

Use 2 tablespoons dipped in water to scoop and form into smooth oval shapes before plating, if desired.

Preheat oven to 325°F. Using a food processor, blend raw livers until smooth. Remove livers and set aside. Blend butter and duck fat until smooth (no need to clean the machine in between). Heat cream in a small saucepan; keep hot on burner.

Add livers back into the processor with the fats and purée until smooth. While the machine is running, add egg yolks, one at a time. Gradually add hot cream to the mixture while still running the food processor.

Press mixture through a mesh sieve into a bowl; discard any liquid. Whisk in brandy, salt, and white pepper. Pour mixture into a terrine mould (a loaf pan will work well). Place the mould into a water bath (a deep, ovenproof pan filled with boiling water, about halfway up the sides of the terrine). Place the terrine into the preheated oven; cook until internal temperature of 130°F is reached when using a quick-read thermometer, or for about 30 minutes.

Remove the terrine from oven and allow to chill thoroughly, then cover with plastic wrap and place in the refrigerator for at least 4 hours to set.

Serve scooped from the terrine and placed into ramekins or small jars, plated with toasted baguette slices, grainy mustard, pickled radish slices, cornichon, and microgreens.

Garnishes can also include wine jelly, shallot marmalade, and fresh figs.

Rebecca Hunt

Chef, Picnic PEC

The first food truck in the County is now also a beloved full-service catering company & café.

I was born and raised in the Thousand Islands, just a little east of the County. I lived in Toronto for twenty years. Got married there. Bought a house and then sold the house and moved here, because I wanted to relax and have a bit more casual way of living. I'd been working as a documentary production manager, and my husband, Stew, left his union job at Molson to pursue his art full-time. ¶ I worked in restaurants from a very young age, always front of house. I worked at a French bistro, one of the first vegetarian restaurants in Toronto, called Citron. And then I went to France and worked at a bed and breakfast. ¶ I wanted to buy an Airstream and have a little espresso and baguette, sandwich, Parisian roadside kind of thing. And then I saw how expensive they were. But that led to the food truck. I'd been in the County for a couple months, and it was 5:00 a.m. and I couldn't sleep. I needed to research this food truck thing to see if it was even possible. So I Googled "food truck Prince Edward County" and the very first thing that popped up was this contest to win a food truck, and I took it as a sign. ¶ I won the truck. Well, I won $15,000 toward a $65,0000 truck. So basically, I inherited a huge amount of debt. But it got me on the map. ¶ I like it when I get to do new things. We have items on the menu that stay relatively the same, but I like changing it up and seeing what looks good at the markets. I mostly work with Edwin County Farms and Blue Wheelbarrow; Aaron's very open to working with chefs to grow the stuff we need. Otherwise, I drive around and I'll ask questions, or I'll post on Facebook. Not every farm stand has the same stuff every week, so you have to look around a little. ¶ Our café opened August 1, 2019. It was tough to open during the busy season of the year, which is also my busiest season for my catering side. My cousin had just moved here and he wanted a job, so he ran the place for the first three months while I was behind the scenes. ¶ At the moment, I use the food truck quite a bit less, which was the intention. Food trucks do really well in places like San Francisco and Miami because their season is ten to twelve months. Here it's three to four months, if you're lucky. Our bricks-and-mortar space is open seven days a week all through the year, to offset having this crazy spike in my schedule every summer from doing the food truck. Right now, I'm just using the food truck for big events, music festivals, the odd wedding, just stuff I want to do.

MEZZE PLATTER

This is something that could be whipped up at a cottage and grazed on all day, or as a healthy and flavourful lunch, or set out as a canapé platter at a party. It's kind of a throw-together-whatever-canned-and-fresh-goodies-that-work-well-together meal.

GREEN TAHINI DIP

¾ cup cilantro

¾ cup parsley

1 cup tahini

¼ cup lemon juice

dash cumin, salt, and pepper

Mix all ingredients in a blender, taste. Drizzle in cold water in ¼-cup increments until you reach the flavour and consistency you like—I love it thick for a sandwich spread, but a little runnier as a dip or sauce to go over roasted vegetables.

BURNT EGGPLANT DIP

2 medium eggplants

½ cup tahini

1 tbsp pomegranate molasses

1 tbsp lemon juice

pinch dried sumac

⅓ cup parsley and mint, combined (optional)

salt and pepper to taste

Roast a couple of eggplants over an open flame (I like to use a hibachi, but a gas element works too). When skin looks black all the way around, remove from heat and let cool. Peel eggplant and discard skins; place in blender with rest of ingredients. Season with salt and pepper to taste.

ROASTED RED PEPPER AND FETA DIP

1 can fire-roasted red peppers

¼ cup olive oil

1½ cups feta cheese
(goat or sheep is the tastiest)

2 roasted garlic cloves

To roast garlic, peel away papery outer layers, leaving individual skins intact; cover whole head in oil and cook at 400°F in a toaster oven for 30 minutes (keep the rest of the head on hand for other recipes). Whip ingredients on high in a food processor until you like the consistency, about 5 minutes.

QUICK PICKLED CAULIFLOWER, BEETS, OR CARROTS

1 cup rice vinegar

½ cup water

½ cup white sugar

Place all ingredients together in a pot and heat until sugar is dissolved; no need to boil it. Let cool. Place vegetable (cauliflower, beets, or carrots) in a glass jar and cover with pickling liquid. You should do this at least 2 hours ahead, preferable the day before. Vegetables keep for 1 week done in this method.

To serve, use all or as many of the below options as you like! Enjoy with friends or keep it all to yourself—you worked hard for this.

• Roasted red peppers, canned or homemade

• Any kind of olive (the more types, the better!); sun-dried kalamata are my favourite

• Lightly grilled halloumi cheese and/or sliced feta and/or ricotta salata

• Sliced cucumber, radish, cherry tomatoes, endive, blanched green beans, or peas

• Quick pickled cauliflower, beets, or carrots

• Roasted zucchini: slice thinly, lightly oil, and salt; roast at 375°F for 10 minutes

• Grilled pita—brush pita with olive oil, salt, and pepper—and green thyme or za'atar; heat a heavy skillet over medium-high heat, grill pitas individually until charred in spots, about 2 minutes per side

• Crackers/crostini

For a meal version, turn your mezze platter into a bowl. Short-grain brown rice is my go-to; it has a nice texture and nutty flavour, with more nutritional density than a basmati or white rice. Layer warm and cool ingredients on top of the rice—a variety of textures and temperatures is best.

> Dips can all be prepared a day ahead and will keep for about 1 week, but they won't last that long anyway.

Lee Arden Lewis

Entrepreneur; Chef, most recently at Jackson's Falls Inn & Restaurant
Reflections from a multi-talented entrepreneur & musings about what she'll do next.

I was born in Belleville, Ontario, the youngest of eight, a proud wharf rat. I loved creating foods from a young age and was always hanging around a kitchen somewhere. I used to go to the Legion because I knew the ladies were always cooking, and I'd bug them until they let me help them make sandwiches. I found out later that they'd call my mother to let her know where I was. I always thought I was so cool, but my mom always knew where I was. ¶ My mother's family emigrated from Scotland and my father's family is of Mohawk descent. When I was in grade school, I'd go to my grandparents' place for lunch every school day. Monday through Thursday we had Papa Lou's corn soup and pan bread in a cast-iron skillet. Fridays, my grandmother made hot dogs with steamed buns. ¶ I dropped out of school after Grade 10. I was always one for an adventure and I knew I could always get a job in a kitchen. I tried college for a short time, but I just couldn't sit in a classroom. ¶ I spent some time out west and ran a little restaurant in Florida for a bit, while I was working as a carny. Sold wholesale foods for Andy Williams and got to know a different level of the food world doing that. Moved back to Canada, started an organic herb farm in Waupoos before it was cool. It was one of several County businesses that got together and helped get Taste the County up and running to market Prince Edward County. And then the County exploded. ¶ I was also parenting and being a mother. For years, I did contract work with Native territories and Ottawa for federal government departments, working on Indigenous initiatives. I became a liaison for the Federal Communications Commission in Washington. My last contract was helping friends market their elk meat here in the County. ¶ The County has always been home. My children's great-grandfather was the first cheesemaker at Black River Cheese in 1901. ¶ Originally, I was going to use Jackson's Falls to do culinary tours in the County. And then my friend Peter, who owned the inn at the time, died suddenly. I was working at Harvest as a bartender and I thought, "I'm gonna buy this place." I had no idea how I'd get the money, but I did. I figured it out. It's taken everything I have to build this place. But I love the ability to be creative and be surrounded by people coming and going. ¶ I think walking away from Jackson's Falls, I'll need some time to think about what I want to do next. I want to create. I see creating and adventure in my future. ¶ The recipes I've shared here are from fond memories of a fortunate childhood.

SUMAC BAKED BANNOCK

5 cups flour

2½ tbsp baking powder

1 tbsp salt

1 tbsp dried sumac

4 cups water

Preheat oven to 400°F. Add about 2 tablespoons of vegetable oil to the bottom of a 12-inch cast-iron skillet; place in oven to heat.

In a large bowl, sift flour, baking powder, salt, and sumac. Add water gradually to the dry ingredients, mixing gently until the dry ingredients are wet. Do not overmix.

Take the hot cast-iron skillet out of the oven and add the bannock mix, spreading it evenly into the pan. Bake for 45 minutes, checking doneness with a sharp knife inserted in the centre; if there's no batter remaining on the knife, it's ready. Turn onto a cooling rack and enjoy!

MOHAWK LYED CORN SOUP

2 cups dried navy beans

2 large fresh or smoked pork hocks, skin on (approximately 4 lbs)

2 tbsp vegetable oil

2 cups chopped cooking onion

3 tbsp chopped garlic

12 cups water

2 cups lyed corn

salt and pepper to taste

Lyed corn can be purchased at the Free Flow Gas Bar (with the Subway Sandwich shop) on Highway 49 in Tyendinaga Mohawk Territory.

Cover the beans with water and soak overnight.

In a large stock pot, add the oil, and over medium-high heat, sear the pork hocks for about 15 minutes. Remove from pot. Add the onions and garlic to the pot and sauté until translucent and just browned. Add the pork hocks back to the pot and cover with water (approximately 12 cups). Bring to a boil and simmer until the meat begins to fall off the bones. Remove the pork hocks from the pot and set aside to cool.

Drain the soaked beans and add to the pot, with additional water to cover if needed. Bring to a boil and simmer until the beans become soft, about 25 minutes.

Rinse the lyed corn with cold water. Add the corn to the pot and simmer for 10 minutes.

Take the meat off the pork hock bones, discard the skin, and chop the meat. Add the meat to the pot and taste for seasoning. Add salt and pepper to taste.

For added depth of flavour, I sometimes season fresh pork hocks with salt and pepper, and slow roast in an oven at 220°F for several hours until browned, before adding to the soup pot.

Luhana & Zach Littlejohn

Farmers, Littlejohn Farm

A sustainably focused farm offering workshops & corporate team-building experiences.

We met when we were getting ready to walk the Camino de Santiago in Spain. We started talking, started walking together, and thirty-four days later we decided to go together to Lu's hometown in northeast Brazil. We moved to Toronto together after Lu finished her master's in microfinance. ¶ Before we came to Prince Edward County, we knew we wanted a place that had a good blend of both agriculture and tourism. You can't find too many rural communities in Canada that have such great restaurants, good coffee. We're pretty spoiled. I think the diversity is what attracted us to the area. ¶ We specialize in culinary-based workshops, wine tours, and corporate team-building to teach people where their food comes from with wholesome, healthy, and sustainable cuisine. We market to companies in the major cities; they bring out their team, and we get them to work together in creating a beautiful meal from our farm. And then everyone sits down and explains what they learned. ¶ We ran an Airbnb farm stay for the last couple of years, and 2019 was the last season we did the farm stay. We're taking our house back. ¶ The property is three and a half acres. When we were putting our plans on paper, doing our research, everyone talked about having hundred-acre plots. But when we asked them how much of the land they actually used, most people were like, "Oh, we have seven to thirteen acres of workable land." And so we settled on a small plot that's right in the heart of cash-crop farming. ¶ We show people when they come that you don't need much to make an impact. You can grow a lot in a really small space. We've gone with a very low-density planting model because we are giving ourselves a chance to grow into our farming. ¶ If we did high-density planting, we'd grow way more food than we could ever use at this point. And we can always try and become suppliers, but then we would outgrow that business model pretty quickly too. Our model doesn't give us the time to spend every Saturday selling veggies at farmers' markets. Now, if we need to scale, we can always plant another row of beets, another row of carrots, depending on how the bookings are coming in on the season. ¶ We started out aiming to produce all our own food. This year, pretty much all of the events that we did, with the exception of seafood, we were able to provide ourselves. ¶ The crazy thing about this area is that the season is so concentrated, and in the twenty-five weeks you just don't have a chance to look up. And sometimes we find ourselves doing jobs that we never thought we would do. ¶ Zach's dad has been a great resource. He comes from an old-school farming background, while obviously we take a little bit of a new-age approach where we're like, okay, we're not farming a thousand acres, and the quality of products is what we're going after, instead of going after high yields. I would rather clip and prune and have better-quality melons, fewer melons that are the best melons you've ever had rather than have tons of melons that taste like pig food. We try to meet somewhere in the middle.

COCKEREL COOKED IN SHERRY CREAM

Cockerel

1 large cockerel, divided
into 4 pieces (or roasting chicken)

3 leeks, sliced

1 stalk celery, sliced

1 carrot, sliced

3 garlic cloves, peeled

1 cup Oloroso sherry

1 L chicken stock

1 tbsp Littlejohn Farm honey

100 ml 35% whipping cream

2 tbsp all-purpose flour

pinch of salt

3 cranks of black pepper

1 bunch sage

3 tbsp sunflower seed oil

Sourdough Biscuits

1 stick or ¼ lb cold,
unsalted butter

1½ cups all-purpose flour

2 tsp baking powder

1 tsp kosher salt

¼ cup Littlejohn Farm
sourdough starter

½ cup whole milk

1 egg (for egg wash)

¾ cup grated cheddar cheese
(optional)

½ chopped green onion
(optional)

To prepare the cockerel, preheat oven to 350°F. Lightly coat poultry in all-purpose flour. Heat a large cast-iron skillet on high heat with sunflower oil. Sear each piece of poultry until golden brown. Remove chicken from pan and set aside. Add vegetables, sage, and garlic. Lightly stir for 1 minute. Deglaze with sherry and honey, reduce by half.

Transfer to a Dutch oven. Add chicken stock and bring to a simmer. Cover pot and place in oven for 2½ hours. (If using a more tender roasting chicken, reduce oven cooking time from 2½ hours to about 1 hour, or until chicken is tender and fully cooked.) Remove pot and allow to cool for 30 minutes. Strain liquid and reduce by half. Add cream in thirds while continuing to reduce. Season with salt and pepper. The sauce is finished once it comfortably coats the back of a spoon. Dress pieces of poultry in sauce and plate.

Enjoy with our signature sourdough biscuits. To prepare biscuits, preheat oven to 400°F and line a baking sheet with parchment paper. Whisk together flour, baking powder, and salt in a large bowl. Toss butter into the dry ingredients until coated with flour. Working quickly, using your fingers or a pastry blender, cut butter into flour until it resembles coarse meal. Transfer to a large bowl. Add cheese and green onion, if using. Combine milk and sourdough starter, and stir with a fork until it just comes together into a slightly sticky, shaggy dough. For small biscuits, use a teaspoon to mound walnut-sized balls of dough; for large biscuits, use a ¼-cup measuring scoop to mound balls of dough onto prepared baking sheet. Brush biscuits with egg wash and bake until golden brown, about 15 minutes for small biscuits and 20 minutes for large ones. Let cool slightly, then transfer to wire rack. Serve warm or at room temperature.

Sas Long

Farmer, Floralora Flowers

A seasonally inspired floral design studio & sustainably run flower farm.

I moved to Prince Edward County in 2012. I was working in Toronto as Ruth Gangbar's assistant, doing food styling, and it was Ruth who introduced me to the County. I moved out here to work at Vicki's Veggies, and it was through my time that first summer that I fell totally in love with this place. I started working there in May, and at the end of August, my mom got sick with cancer and I had to leave the County to take care of her. Within six weeks of finding out she had cancer, she died. ¶ I took a year off to deal with my mom's affairs and travel, but when I left, I'd already decided that Prince Edward County was my new home and I wanted to start my own endeavour here—I'm one of those people who really loves to have their own business. ¶ I decided to grow flowers. They were a passion of mine, and nobody was really growing flowers in the area. Prince Edward County was changing, and it just felt like a missing niche. The wedding craze came later, which has sealed the deal as the right place at the right time. I came back and rented an acre from Quinta do Conde, right on the Black River. I planted an acre of flowers and sold them at markets in Toronto, and ran a flower subscription in the County. And then somebody asked me to do a wedding. Over the next few years, alongside growing flowers, I dove into learning how to do floral design. The wedding part of the business has grown more than I ever expected because now the County is a major wedding destination, and we have something unique to offer. ¶ The first year I worked by myself, and the second year saw a major expansion when I bought my current property with my sister. She bought the field that I grow in and I bought the house on a couple of acres. We have six and a half acres altogether. ¶ I think sometimes you have an idea of what your business is going to be, and then you actually do it and it totally changes. I thought I'd grow flowers and sell them at markets, or through subscriptions, and that would be it. And then I just kept growing more and more and more flowers, and I needed to sell them all. So I started selling wholesale to florists in Toronto, and took on a couple grocery stores there as well. I'd never thought of selling at a large chain like Sobeys, but our flowers have done super well there. ¶ Flower farming isn't dreamy and romantic all the time. It can just be straight-up hard work. It can also be very demanding to balance everything that comes with owning a business, like marketing, paperwork, bookkeeping. ¶ My learning process is never-ending. I got a great foundation by working for other farmers and I did a ton of research of my own. I'll continue to learn through trial and error, and growing new things all the time.

FLOURLESS CHOCOLATE CAKE

4 oz fine-quality bittersweet chocolate (not unsweetened)

1 stick (½ cup) unsalted butter, plus more for greasing pan

¾ cup sugar

3 large eggs

½ cup unsweetened cocoa powder, plus more for sprinkling

Preheat oven to 375°F and butter an 8-inch round springform baking pan. Line with a round of parchment or buttered wax paper.

Chop chocolate into small pieces. In a double boiler, or metal bowl set over a saucepan of simmering water, melt chocolate with butter, stirring until smooth.

Remove top of double boiler or bowl from heat and whisk sugar into chocolate mixture. Add eggs and whisk well. Sift cocoa powder over chocolate mixture and whisk until just combined.

Pour batter into prepared pan and bake in middle of oven for 20 to 25 minutes, or until top has formed a thin crust. Cool cake in pan on a rack for 5 minutes, then remove to serving plate by inverting or sliding carefully off bottom of pan.

Dust cake with icing sugar or cocoa powder; garnish with edible flowers and fruit, if desired.

Jennifer McCaw

Baker, Farmhouse Eats at Hagerman Farms
Family-run century farm located just outside of Picton with a seasonal farm stand & bakery.

Grandma and Grandpa started by selling potatoes and tomatoes from a tiny stand. They also put in a dairy dip across the road as a way to earn a little extra money. I've seen pictures of the five-cent cones they used to sell and local families used to come down once a week to buy. Because that's what they could afford as a treat. ¶ Growing up, we ate simple homemade meals from food provided by our own fields, like corn, potatoes, tomatoes, and cucumbers. We also grew pumpkin and squash. For years, we picked pumpkins with a pitchfork, and slung them into a tractor trailer. After a while, we decided to invest in a pumpkin picker so we could sell more pumpkins to the canning factory. And as soon as our picker arrived from the States, the factory closed. ¶ We went into fresh-market vegetables in a big way. And then we started the bakery in 2012 and worked out of the house kitchen. We thought of it as a trial year and put out a display case and a little shelf of jam at the stand. It got busy to the point where we were selling out of baked goods and prepared food by noon. We couldn't keep up. ¶ It's good work, it's rewarding, but some days are tough. In the summer, it's usually ten-hour days, six days a week. That's why we generally shut down in the off-season, except for a few big orders for baking. When we shut down, we spend a few weeks stripping stuff down and scrubbing the entire place. And then we go ice fishing all winter. ¶ The main thing to know about the business is that it's a family affair. You're with family every day. The best part of the job is working with the people you love and being able to work where we grew up. And there's an endless supply of learning when it comes to food. ¶ Everyone shops at the farm, from low-income families to tourists looking for a higher-end country market. We do our best to provide a little something for each group of people. It's a tricky balance but it's important to serve everybody.

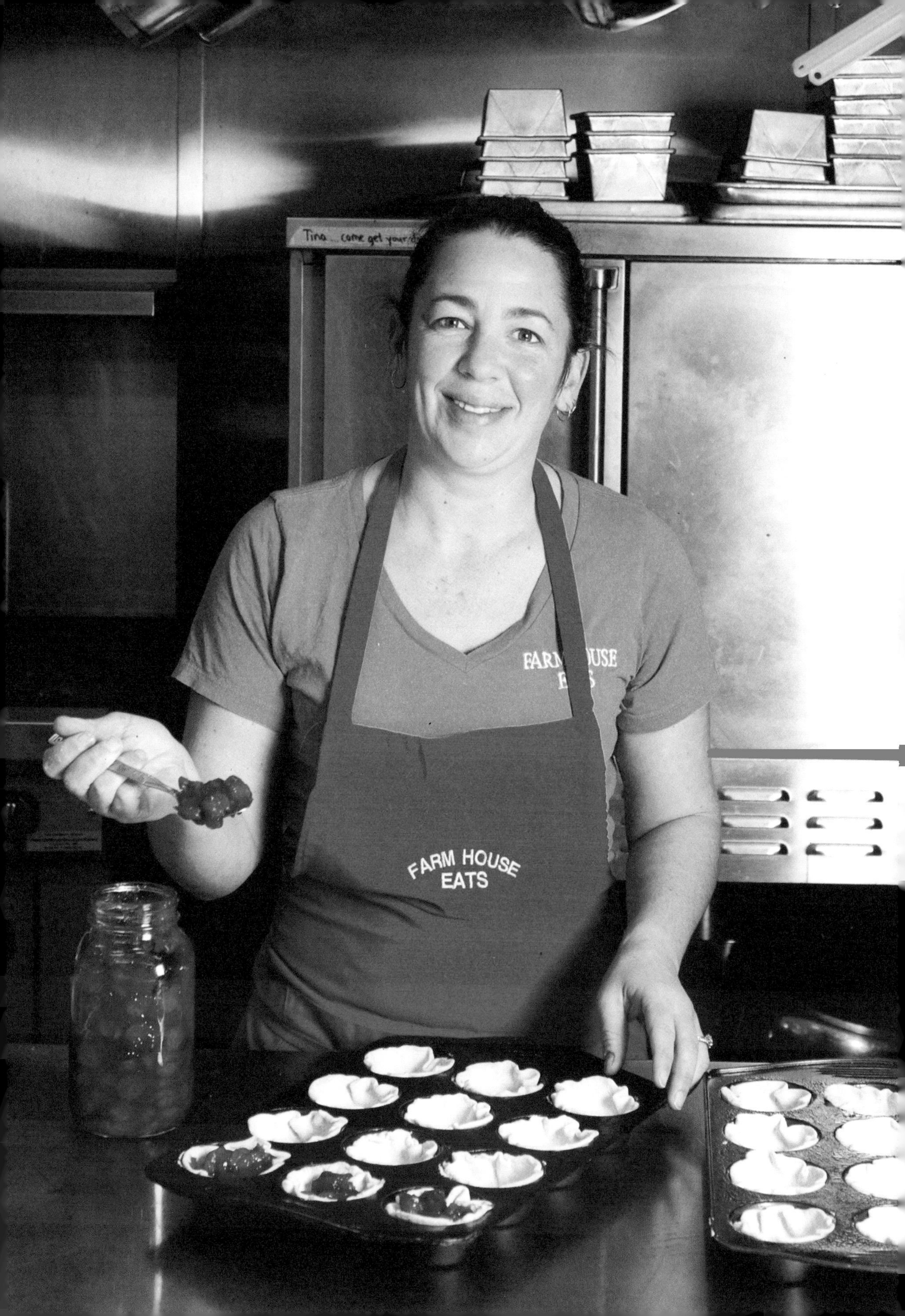
FARM HOUSE
EATS

BLUEBERRY SHORTCAKES

8 cups all-purpose flour

2 cups white sugar,
plus extra for sprinkling

⅓ cup baking powder

1½ tsp baking soda

1½ tsp salt

2 cups vegetable shortening

3–4 cups fresh buttermilk

1 cup fresh blueberries
(washed and dried)

1 egg yolk

1 tbsp table cream

This bakeshop recipe generously makes about 24 large biscuits, but can be halved easily.

Preheat oven to 350°F. Combine flour, sugar, baking powder, baking soda, and salt in a large mixing bowl.

Use a pastry cutter to blend shortening into dry ingredients, until you have pea-sized pieces.

Make a large well in the centre of blended ingredients. Add blueberries and 3 cups buttermilk.

Use a bench scraper to mix until you have a roughly formed dough ball. If it falls apart, add buttermilk a small amount at a time, being careful not to overmix.

Flour surface and roll dough ball out of bowl. Roll to roughly 1 to 1½-inch thick and cut with round cookie cutter (or glass).

Line shortcakes on parchment-covered baking sheet. Combine egg yolk and table cream for egg wash. Brush shortcakes with egg wash and sprinkle generously with extra sugar.

Bake at 350°F for 20 to 25 minutes.

Enjoy with whipped cream and local seasonal berries or toasted with vanilla ice cream.

Gavin North & Bay Woodyard

Beekeepers, Honey Pie Hives & Herbals
A wonderful, whimsical small bee & herb farm & natural products shop.

We bought our first bees in 2000. There was a steep learning curve, and we found within the first couple of years that we had to gain a lot of experience to manage the business and we had to deal with mites and winter bee losses much higher than we had been told about. ¶ We also found right away that there was a certain group of people in the County interested in buying our products. But it was a very, very small sliver of people. There wasn't really the concept yet that you would pay more for something that was handmade. We knew our customers were out there, but we had to go and find them and market to them. ¶ It's been a continual process of learning about bees and herbal products, figuring out how to combine honey, beeswax, and plants to make herbal salves, herbal teas, and balms. ¶ We love the creative aspect of developing new products and making up new recipes. We hear a few whispers from people about a product they're looking for and then we dive into the research until we decide, okay, it's time to make this thing. ¶ We mostly try to use things that we can grow, or use plants that already grow wild on our property. Our business totally shifted from the early days from what sounds like fun to make to what is actually environmentally friendly and natural. ¶ We're part of a Slow Food movement that's all about preserving food culture in local areas around the world. It's up to every local chapter to determine what their local food culture is and how to preserve it. ¶ There's a new group that has sprung out of Slow Food, called Slow Bees. It's all about educating people about climate change through bees. It started with asking people to plant flowering trees for bees. And to avoid using insecticides—or eating foods sprayed with insecticides. ¶ We don't actually believe that more is better. Small is beautiful. And if we scale our business back so that we're not as exhausted, we can actually offer more to our community, working with people to plant more trees and to promote Slow Bees and teach classes about how to make things by hand.

HAZELNUT HONEY BUCKWHEAT BROWNIES

These brownies are gluten-free and can be easily adapted to be dairy-free. We make these brownies using hazelnuts from our own trees.

¾ cup hazelnuts, toasted and ground

1 cup butter

¾ cup honey

¾ cup cocoa

2 eggs

½ tsp vanilla

½ tsp salt

½ cup buckwheat flour

Preheat oven to 350°F. Spread hazelnuts on a baking sheet and bake for 10 to 15 minutes, until they are lightly toasted and their skins crack. Remove from oven and rub off skins between two clean dishtowels. Grind toasted hazelnuts in a food processor fitted with a steel blade (or chop with a knife), until they are coarsely chopped. Set aside.

Melt butter in small saucepan over low heat. Add honey and cocoa and whisk with melted butter to combine. Let cool a little, then transfer to a medium-sized bowl.

Add eggs, vanilla, and salt; stir to combine. Stir in buckwheat flour and beat with an electric mixer (or very briskly with a hand whisk), for 2 minutes.

Stir in ground hazelnuts and spread into a parchment paper-lined 8-inch square or a lightly greased 9-inch round ovenproof glass pie plate. Bake for 25 to 30 minutes, until a toothpick comes out clean when placed in the centre.

Tim Noxon

Farmer/Food Producer, Mirepoix Farm

Seed-to-table organic grower & producer of fine herbs, condiments & hot sauces.

Mirepoix is the name of a town in France. It's also a common cooking term that often refers to carrots, onions, and celery used to make a base for a soup. I like to think of it as a reference to a collection of things that make food taste better. So I took the liberty of adopting the name. ¶ We used to grow a lot of different vegetables, including hot peppers, and for years I really wanted to make hot sauce. Then a colleague I worked with told me about how his grandmother in the Azores made hot sauce through fermenting it, and I thought, "Oh, that sounds good!" So we tried a little test! ¶ It dawned on me that we can grow the peppers, prepare and ferment them, let the pepper mash age, and then process them further in the winter when there's lots of time. It's a good way to keep employees busy through the winter too. The ability to offer year-round employment was definitely one of the factors for adding hot sauce into the mix. ¶ Specializing is the key in farming because the margins are so small. Hot sauce is a non-perishable product; it'll keep for years and just get better. ¶ We have four plots where we rotate crops to isolate certain peppers and save the seed. Some of our peppers are quite rare, and very few folks in Canada are growing them. We have to help them acclimatize. Some of them can be very tricky. ¶ We also grow our own garlic and onions for the hot sauces. Those, plus the peppers, are the three main ingredients. I've also been slowly breaking into fine herb growing, culinary herbs for cooking, dried herbs. I think there's a bit of a niche market out there because the quality of these herbs is so much greater than the stuff you often buy in the grocery store. The difference it makes to your cooking is incredible. The only trick is to sell it. ¶ Our best market is specialty food shops and small wineries that don't sell much of anything else other than wine—they seem to be the ones that sell the most hot sauce. ¶ I'm an artist and designer through my formal education. I went to school for eight years, then ended up sitting in an office at a computer and going to meetings every day. It drove me crazy. I came out to the County for a break thirty years ago to help my dad with a restoration job. And I loved it so much that I decided to leave the city pretty much immediately. ¶ I've been organic farming for fifteen years, and the Mirepoix idea has been going for two years. Things are starting to fall into place. We can grow the peppers. We can make the sauce. Now we need to make sure we don't run out, to keep customers happy.

LEFTOVER PRIME RIB & LENTIL SOUP

This is a warm, hearty, and healthy soup. It's a great way to use up leftover roasts, or you can substitute a couple of barbecued bone-in steaks.

1 leftover prime rib roast with at least 3 ribs, plus a couple handfuls of meat, cubed (alternatively, use any roasted beef bones and tender beef cuts)

8 L water

2 medium cippolini onion or equivalent, cut into rings

2 medium shallots, cut into slivers

2 tbsp beef fat, butter, or oil— or combo of all three

4 medium carrots, diced

4 celery sticks, chopped

2 large tomatoes, chopped

3 large cremini mushrooms, cut into sticks

1 cup French/Puy lentils

2 tsp sea salt

1 good pinch of Mirepoix Farm sweet smoked paprika

1 good pinch of Mirepoix Farm chili flakes

1 good pinch of Mirepoix Farm dried savoury or thyme leaves

black pepper to taste

fresh cilantro leaves and lime juice for serving

Trim the majority of meat off the rib bones and set aside. In a large stock pot, cover bones with water and bring to boil. Skim off any foam and lower heat to simmer for about 1½ hours. Allow to reduce by about half, skimming off fat from top.

Cube any leftover meat into ½-inch squares. In a skillet, sauté half the onions and shallots in fat until softened and beginning to brown. Add to stock pot.

Add remaining ingredients to pot and continue cooking for 45 to 60 minutes. Add water if necessary while cooking. The finished consistency should be half soup/half stew-like.

Adjust salt to taste. Serve in bowls with a good pinch of cilantro and a squeeze of lime as a finish. Add a splash of sriracha-like hot sauce, if desired, and enjoy!

Albert Ponzo

Chef, The Royal Hotel

Albert is living his dream of opening a farm-to-table restaurant in the County.

The first language I learned was Italian. My parents had just moved here from Italy, and my dad hunted. He fished. He had his own garden. Everything was done at home. I grew up in a very family-oriented, around-the-table environment. I always loved food. ¶ I went to college for music and I started playing jazz bass. I loved it. But I couldn't really make ends meet, so I served tables to earn money on the side. ¶ I started loving being in a restaurant, and decided I wanted to open my own. I was around twenty-four, so I was old to go to culinary school—or impatient, one or the other. I wanted to stay in the new, dynamic environment I'd found in the day-to-day restaurant life. I met Didier Leroy, a French chef, through my brother. Didier sent me to a really good restaurant, where I started working for free. ¶ There's a relationship between making music and being in a kitchen. You own your skills, there's camaraderie, and you're performing every night. I ended up moving quickly through the ranks. I'd practise—if a chef yelled at me for cutting chives wrong, on the way home from work I'd buy ten bunches of chives. I thought, "I'm gonna learn how to cut these chives, and I'll show them." ¶ I was brought on at Le Sélect Bistro, a well-known restaurant in Toronto, as executive sous-chef, to support another chef. I was twenty-nine at the time. And then that chef left before he even started. So when the time came to hire, they offered me the job. I went home and talked it over with Marlise, my wife. She asked me what was the worst that could happen if I failed—that the only thing I'd regret was a missed opportunity to chase my dream. So I took it. ¶ We used to visit Prince Edward County at least once a year, and as I started falling in love with farm-to-table cooking, getting more into knowing where my ingredients came from, we talked about moving here. ¶ I was introduced to the Sorbara family by one of the architects working on the Royal Hotel. I cooked for them, and they hired me. It was a perfect fit. We moved our family here. And we haven't looked back since. ¶ Canada is amazing. We have so much to offer here in terms of food. I used to believe that everything is better in Italy—until I tried one of Vicki Emlaw's tomatoes and discovered that fresh, beautiful, flavourful food was entirely possible to find here. My dream is to foster a connection to place through food. My end goal is to only use ingredients from here all year round in my cooking. We have so much to celebrate here, and I want to contribute to that.

FRENCH-STYLE OMELETTE

I love making French-style omelettes. Always use high-quality eggs from happy chickens. When filling an omelette, I use seasonal items like cherry tomatoes, basil, and zucchini flowers in summer; hand-rolled chèvre cheese from Fifth Town Artisan Cheese in winter; wild mushrooms in fall; or asparagus and gravlax in the spring. Let your imagination run wild! I tend to stick to only a few ingredients with simple, fresh flavours, as too much filling makes it hard to roll the omelette.

3 large eggs

3 tbsp 35% cream or milk

1 tbsp extra-virgin olive oil

½ tbsp unsalted butter

2–3 tbsp filling of choice

salt to taste

Whisk eggs, cream, and salt together in a mixing bowl until homogeneous. Heat an 8-inch non-stick pan over high heat.

Work quickly. This whole process should take about a minute. Add olive oil to coat the pan in a thin layer, being careful not to burn oil but ensuring it's very hot. Add butter, which will melt and begin frothing. Add egg mixture, reduce heat to medium, and begin moving the eggs in the pan with a non-stick spatula, allowing the spatula to touch the bottom of the pan in a smooth circular motion so the eggs to cook evenly. As you're cooking the eggs, you will see the last bottom layer forming into one piece like an envelope, which will be continuously broken and re-formed. Once the eggs are 60 to 70 percent cooked, remove the pan from heat and give the omelette one last reform, cleaning the sides of the pan with the spatula. Bang the pan down on a flat, hard surface to create a smooth texture on the bottom.

Add filling ingredients to the middle of the omelette. Change your grip on the pan to an overhand grip. Using the spatula, start folding the omelette from the side closest to the handle of the pan in roughly one-third toward the other end of the pan. Once the omelette is folded, allow the other side of the omelette to touch the plate, where it will act as a fulcrum—allowing you to fold the already folded side of the omelette onto the plate. The omelette will gently pivot as it spins to the plate to complete the last fold or roll. Serve hot with fresh sourdough bread and a green salad.

Michael Potters

Chef, most recently Executive Director of Culinary Arts Prince Edward (the CAPE)
Michael was an incredibly talented and accomplished chef whose career spanned decades. We are incredibly sad to share that Michael took his life at his home in Cherry Valley on February 21, 2020, at the age of fifty-nine.

I got started with food because my parents were such terrible cooks. But I wouldn't say that I came from a really poor food background—my grandmother was a very good cook. I grew up in London, Ontario. My first wife was Italian, and she taught me how to cook very, very rustic Italian food. ¶ I cut my teeth in Toronto, and cooked there for twenty years. My favourite job in Toronto was working as a tournant for a French restaurant. Everybody in the kitchen was French, and I was one of two Canadians in there. I spoke no French. Now I speak culinary French very, very well. ¶ After Toronto, I went to the County, in 2002, with my then-wife, Karin Desveaux. We opened the Milford Bistro; at that time, there was nothing in Milford except the Hicks' General Store. I picked mushrooms at the mushroom farm for the first winter because I needed to pay the mortgage. We had a camera crew come up and follow us for sixteen weeks, until we opened the restaurant. Their film won a Gemini. ¶ Karin and I opened Harvest next, but it was a bit ahead of its time for the County. After Harvest was over and Karen and I split up, I worked at Angeline's Inn in Bloomfield for a year. And then I left for eight years. I basically took a consulting trip all around Ontario, doing a whole bunch of stuff I wanted to do: I opened a butcher shop; built and ran a food truck; did a fine-dining restaurant at Hockley Valley Resort; worked on a thoroughbred horse farm for a year. I was GM of Little Inn of Bayfield. I came back to the County because I had friends and community here. I'm fortunate to have a long and really well-rounded career. ¶ I've been pretty lucky because I learned how to cook very well, owned restaurants. So I learned the business side of things. I've always been supermeticulous about service in the restaurant, probably because of my high-end fine-dining background when I was younger. I figured if you didn't know how to serve a table and take care of the customer properly, how can you ever be a chef? ¶ Cooking-wise, I like technique. I still love the alchemy of sauces. Saucier is probably my biggest thing, and butchery too, because when I came out here, Slow Food was still in its infancy. We didn't want to drive to Toronto to get food, and I knew the quality of the ingredients was better than what I had in the city. That's when I met Vicki Emlaw. Dana Vader for lamb. Lynn Leavitt for beef. And I started to develop all these relationships with farmers. ¶ When I did lamb, I'd bring one lamb in. And we did twenty-five portions off the lamb. We did five different cuts on a plate. I came up with all these different ways of creating and using products so that you used up the whole animal. Whole-animal butchery changed me as a cook, changed me as a chef. I like butchering a lot, making sausages. ¶ There's a lot of really good talent in the County right now. I like eating here probably more than I ever have. I like the community here because the community is tight. Without everyone being here, it wouldn't be the County.

CONIGLIO WITH PEPPERONATA & SAUCE DIABLE

Stuffed Rabbit

1¼–3 lbs free-range rabbit, deboned

4 tbsp extra virgin olive oil

3 garlic cloves, sliced

1 tbsp minced onion

6 white button mushrooms, thinly sliced

½ cup fresh white bread crumbs

2 tbsp sage leaves, chopped

1 tbsp rosemary, chopped

3 tbsp parsley, chopped

2 organic egg yolks

5 tbsp Parmesan cheese

½ cup white wine

sea salt and freshly ground black pepper

6 slices prosciutto

Pepperonata

6 tbsp extra-virgin olive oil

1 small onion, peeled and diced

2 garlic cloves, sliced

3 sweet red peppers, roasted and peeled

3 zucchinis, diced

8 plum tomatoes, peeled and seeded

12–16 infornata (or kalamata) olives, pitted

6 basil leaves, roughly chopped

3 tbsp Italian parsley, roughly chopped

sea salt and freshly ground black pepper

Sauce Diable

3 tbsp extra-virgin olive oil

2 shallots, minced

¼ cup champagne vinegar

1 cup white wine

1 tbsp coriander seeds

2 branches tarragon

1 tsp coarsely ground black pepper

2 coarsely chopped plum tomatoes

2 cups chicken stock

½ cup reduced rabbit stock

3 tbsp cold butter, cut into small pieces

Preheat the oven to 375°F. Remove the head, liver, and kidneys from the rabbit, if present. Rinse the rabbit under cold running water and pat dry with paper towels. Debone the rabbit; remove all the bones and leave the rabbit in one piece.

Preheat a heavy-bottomed skillet over medium heat. Add half the olive oil, onion, and sliced garlic, and caramelize lightly. Add the sliced mushrooms and continue to cook until the mushrooms are soft. Remove from heat and put in a mixing bowl with the bread crumbs, herbs, egg yolks, and Parmesan cheese. Deglaze the skillet with white wine, reduce by half, and add the reduced glaze to the stuffing mixture. Mix well and season with salt and pepper.

Place the deboned rabbit skin-side down on a cutting board. Lay slices of prosciutto on top and spread the stuffing down the centre. Roll into a tight roulade and tie with butcher twine. Season the rabbit lightly with salt and pepper.

Preheat a heavy-bottomed skillet over high heat, add the remaining olive oil, reduce the heat to low, and sear the rabbit until lightly brown. Put the skillet with the rabbit in the oven and roast for 10 to 12 minutes, basting with the pan juices and rotating the pan to brown evenly. Check the temperature of the rabbit by inserting an instant-read thermometer into the centre of the roulade; the temperature should read approximately 130°F. Remove from the oven and baste several times with its pan juices. Let sit in a warm spot for about 10 minutes before carving (the rabbit will continue to cook as it sits, reaching a temperature of about 140°F).

For the pepperonata, preheat a heavy-bottomed skillet over medium heat. Add half of the olive oil, and sauté the onion and garlic until softened. Add the peppers, zucchini, and plum tomatoes. Reduce the heat to low, cover and braise the pepperonata for 10 to 12 minutes with the lid slightly ajar. Add the olives, basil, and parsley. Season with salt and freshly ground black pepper. Remove from heat, allow to cool slightly, and swirl in the remaining extra-virgin olive oil.

For the sauce diable, preheat a saucepan. Add the olive oil and sweat the shallots over medium-low heat. Deglaze the saucepan with champagne vinegar and white wine. Add the coriander seeds, tarragon branches, and coarsely ground black pepper, then reduce until almost dry. Add the tomatoes, chicken stock, and rabbit stock; reduce the sauce until it coats the back of a spoon. Strain through a fine-meshed chinois without pressing and return to a clean saucepan. Place over low heat and whisk in the butter slowly until incorporated.

Carve the rabbit by cutting off the strings and slicing it into ¼-inch slices. Serve on top of the pepperonata, and spoon over the sauce diable.

Steve Purtelle

Chef/President, The Acoustic Grill & Acoustic Jam Records
A cozy pub that offers great beer, great food & the best live acoustic music.

My family owned a little sub shop when I was in high school. We made subs and pizzas, and it was an ice cream shop too in the summertime. And I worked at a bakery when I was in high school. I've always been part of the food industry in some way. ¶ I'm originally from Picton—I was born in the Picton Hospital. I took radio broadcasting at Loyalist in Belleville, and I used to have my own deejay business. I did weddings and parties at Isaiah Tubbs and deejayed at the Hayloft. And then I started working at the golf course grill. I've always had multiple things going on at once. ¶ We opened the Acoustic Grill in 2005. We've always had live music. I've been helping musicians get gigs at other places, which turned into a booking agency. So now I book a few bands across the country. ¶ I found it very hard in the beginning to balance family life and hospitality, because you have to put in so many hours. But the kids have grown up with the business. And they love it. They both work at the Grill when they come home from school. It's a lot easier now that they're older. But it was hard at the start. ¶ My favourite part of hospitality, obviously, is the customers. I love to serve people. The best part is when people tell me how much they love our flatbreads, which I bake myself. Every pint of Guinness that I pour, I put a shamrock on top. And people will say, "You don't really do that all the time, do you?" Every pint of Guinness I've poured in the last fourteen years I've put a shamrock on. Every single time. And I always will. When people notice the little things, that's my favourite part. It makes it worth it to get up at 5:00 a.m., because somebody noticed. ¶ I love the baking. The hours are a little strange, not necessarily because I have to do it early in the morning, because I love doing it early in the morning. But it's really time-consuming and there are no shortcuts in baking. You have to wait. There's an amount of time it takes to make a batch of buns or flatbreads or bread. And you can't change that. So that can be a little challenging. ¶ Jenny and I got together fairly soon after the Acoustic Grill opened, so she's been there through the entire thing. The structure of the Grill is that Jenny handles front of house and I handle back of house, but we basically do everything together. We enjoy working together. We always have. Friends warned me that relationships don't last in hospitality. It's true, they don't. But Jenny and I have always gotten along well. ¶ It'll be hard to let the Acoustic Grill go. This place is my dream. And I don't want to sell it. But I'm also a businessman. And at some point, it'll be the right time to move on. ¶ If I could do it all again I wouldn't change anything. You grow from the mistakes you make. I think I've learned a lot from making mistakes. It would be boring to do everything perfectly. So I wouldn't change anything.

BLUE CHEESE DRESSING

I love chicken wings! I love all meats in all forms, but the chicken wing is special. Once considered a throwaway by many chefs, wings are now a staple of any pub menu. What I love the most are the potentially endless variations, but the best is blue cheese. So here's my homemade blue cheese dressing that we serve at the Acoustic Grill.

4 cups blue cheese (crumbled)

2 cups sour cream

4 cups mayonnaise

1 cup lemon juice

½ cup honey

1 tbsp minced garlic

salt and pepper to taste

This recipe makes enough to feed a large, hungry crowd, but it halves (or even quarters) easily enough.

Combine all ingredients in a large bowl. Mix gently. Do not blend—the chunks are important.

Scott Royce

Chef, Seasoned Events; Instructor, Loyalist College Culinary Program
Full-service catering & unique pop-up dinner events.

I grew up just outside of Toronto, in Markham, Ontario. My interest in food started at a young age, cooking with my father. My dad was the cook in our family. Dinner was our time together around the table each night. ¶ Sitting still in school wasn't my thing. When it came time for post-secondary decisions, my dad encouraged me to give cooking a try. I got a job at the local Italian eatery and went to George Brown College right out of high school. At the Italian eatery I remember my first exposure to a busy lunch: the sound of the chit machine, the chatter in the dining room. We were slinging pizzas in the wood-burning oven, tossing pastas with house sauces. During service, I headed frantically to the walk-in fridge to restock my station, and remember grabbing for the door handle, standing on the checkered plate covering the grease trap, and thinking, "I love this!" And that's where I fell in love with the adrenaline, teamwork, precision, organization, and execution of service. ¶ My first fine-dining job was at Terra in Thornhill. It was a steep learning curve for me, it was sink or swim. When I entered that kitchen, I had zero comprehension of what the other cooks were doing, or why. Days blew by—there was never enough prep time. I made gnocchi every day in that kitchen. I learned so much there. ¶ I spent some time out west, in Lake Louise and Calgary, before moving to the County in 2006 to help open Harvest with Karin Desveaux and Michael Potters. During my time there, I began to teach part-time at Loyalist College. ¶ After five years at Harvest, I moved on to become the chef at Waupoos Estates Winery for three seasons. Around the time my daughter was born, I landed a full-time position at Loyalist College. I've been there for ten years now. I teach two days a week in Resto 213, running dinner service with twenty or so students. The remainder of my week is spent managing the kitchen and supporting the other chefs in the program. ¶ I met Kyle Otsuka when I was operating my first catering company. I did a catering job for him, and made diagrams for plating and gave very informative step-by-step instructions. Kyle talks about opening up my packaging and saying, "Who is this person?" We became old friends fast and ended up starting Seasoned Events together. Kyle and I work very well together because we have complementing skill sets, and a drive to make everything the best we can. We have developed some really interesting systems together that have landed us in a place where I feel that we have one brain. ¶ I chose to include this dish because it's fresh, light, all about peak County berries. It's an exciting dish for me because it shows wine as a food. Guests at our Seasoned Events pop-ups have really enjoyed the play on sweetness and acidity between the berries and the sparkling wine.

SPARKLING RASPBERRY GELÉE

Raspberry Coulis

1 qt local raspberries

½ cup sugar

½ cup fresh lemon juice

Sparkling Gelée

750 ml your favourite
County sparkling wine

250 ml raspberry coulis

½ cup sugar

7 sheets gelatin, bloomed
in cold water

1 qt local raspberries,
for plating

Almond Tuiles

45 g butter

60 g icing sugar

45 g egg whites

50 g cake flour

a few drops almond extract

100 g slivered almonds

Make the gelée in advance and wow your dinner guests with something a little different. Sweetness can be slightly adjusted to suit your palate or to suit the wine.

To prepare the raspberry coulis, combine all ingredients in a saucepan and simmer for 10 minutes, strain and chill. Reserve half for gelée mix, the other half for plating.

For the gelée, place 350 ml of sparkling wine into a stainless-steel saucepan. Gently heat the sparkling wine over medium heat, until just before it comes to a boil. Dissolve the bloomed gelatin and sugar in the heated wine. In a mixing bowl, temper the hot wine mixture into the remaining wine. Whisk in the raspberry coulis. Hold the mixture at room temperature for assembly.

Add 2 tablespoons of the gelée mix into each cooking oil-sprayed silicone mould. Chill until firm. Cut a few raspberries in half, coat them in the gelée mixture, and place them in the centre of the pre-chilled base. Chill in the refrigerator until firm. Carefully top up the moulds with more of the gelée mix. Chill once more; overnight is best.

For the tuiles, cream the butter and sugar in a mixer fitted with a paddle attachment. Once creamed, beat in the egg whites and almond extract. Mix in the sifted flour by hand until well incorporated.

Using a small palate knife, evenly spread the tuile mixture onto a silicone mat using a circular stencil. Repeat until all of the mixture is used. Place a few almond slivers on each cookie before baking.

Bake at 350°F for about 7 minutes, until the cookies are golden brown. Cool and reserve for plating.

To serve, gently unmould the gelées by placing the moulds in a tray of hot water for a few minutes, until the gelées free up. Plate with layers of fresh berries, tuiles, remaining coulis, and fresh mint to garnish.

Nicholas Sorbara

Farmer, Edwin County Farms; Senior Partner, Redlab Inc.
A 700-acre family farm producing organic vegetables, beef, cereals & maple syrup.

I grew up on a hobby farm. My grandfather was a farmer. I always assumed I'd grow up to be a farmer. In high school, however, I developed an interest in film and production after being the production manager of the high school play. I studied film and television at Concordia but quit after a year, thinking I could either stay three more years and learn about it or I could actually go and do it. I left school, landed a job as a production assistant, and through sheer luck met another guy on the same path as me. In 2007, the two of us started a post-production company called Redlab. We now employ fifty people and have landed some pretty major international TV shows and movies. ¶ While I continue to be a partner at Redlab, my wife and I moved our two daughters to Prince Edward County in 2018. My family had purchased a farm in the County in 2005, and since then I had been spending my weekends here, enjoying all the area had to offer with no thought of farming on our family property. I felt like I was too old and uneducated in farming to bother starting. Then, in September 2017, our family went to Blue Hill at Stone Barns in New York. The first *Chef's Table* was on Dan Barber, the chef at Stone Barns. We did the farm tour and then the kitchen tour and then had dinner. During the farm tour, my family kept saying, "Oh, this is what we can do on our farm, we can do this and that," and the whole time I was thinking, "Who's gonna do that? You're crazy." By the end of it, I thought, "I'm gonna do it." That was the turning point. ¶ When my grandfather was farming, I bet he traded knowledge at church on Sunday or learned from his neighbours and through trial and error. Now we have the internet. I'm certain that in a few short months I had access to more information about farming than my grandfather could have acquired in a lifetime. There's currently a renaissance of young farmers working the land and sharing their knowledge online, whether they're doing it rurally or in cities or wherever. ¶ Last year for us was mostly planting and getting people excited about the farm. It was a real year of learning and figuring out how we were going to do it and why we're doing it. This kind of operation you can run with two or three people and be fairly profitable. You can feed a hotel and a community and some restaurants—which is the other reason I got into vegetable farming—I like good food. ¶ Small-scale farming is the way we're going to save the world—capturing carbon and putting it in the ground. That's enough motivation for me to want to be a farmer. Our family's motto is to always leave a place better than you found it, whether it be the campsite you're on or whenever else, leave it a little bit nicer than you found it. And if everybody does that, then things get better.

BEAN BALLS

The recipe is more of a process than a specific list of carefully measured ingredients, and you should feel free to play around with the ingredients and amounts until you get a result that's uniquely yours.

2 cups of dried soybeans, soaked overnight

1 bay leaf

¼–⅓ cup barley

1 or 2 eggs

1 tbsp barley or brown rice miso

1–2 medium onions, finely chopped

2 garlic cloves, finely chopped

1 celery stalk, finely chopped

6 mushrooms, finely chopped

3–4 sprigs parsley

1 tbsp chopped fresh thyme

1 tbsp chopped fresh sage

4–5 medium carrots, grated

1 medium to medium-large beet, grated

½ cup grated Parmesan

1 can (156 ml) tomato paste (approximately ½ cup)

1 cup bread crumbs (preferably homemade)

sea salt and black pepper to taste

3–4 tbsp any good vegetable oil (olive, safflower, sunflower, canola)

Drain and rinse beans. Place in a large pot with bay leaf; cover with plenty of cold water.

Cover pot with lid; cook over medium-low heat until beans are tender and easily squished between thumb and forefinger. Remove from heat and set aside.

Cook barley covered in water for 30 minutes over medium heat, or until tender and swollen. Remove from heat, drain, and set aside.

Remove bay leaf, drain cooled beans, and place in a food processor or blender. Add eggs and miso. Blend mixture until it forms a smooth paste but is still slightly granular.

In a large bowl, mix together the vegetables and bean mixture. Add Parmesan, tomato paste, cooked barley, bread crumbs, salt, pepper, and oil. Refrigerate and allow mixture to sit for 30 minutes to 1 hour, to allow flavours to meld (and for some of the moisture to be absorbed by the bread crumbs).

Preheat oven to 400°F. Grease, or preferably, line a baking tray with parchment paper.

Oil your hands, grab a small handful of bean mixture, and form into small balls about 2 inches in diameter. (An ice-cream scoop also works well for this). Arrange balls on the baking sheet, leaving an inch or so between them. Drizzle balls with a tiny bit of oil before placing tray in oven. Bake at 400°F for 20 minutes. Reduce heat to 350°F and continue baking for another 20 minutes or until slightly dry and almost crispy on the outside, with a light, moist interior.

These can be served any number of ways. As we are a largely vegetarian family, these were our alternative to turkey at holidays like Christmas and Thanksgiving, where they were usually accompanied by mashed potatoes and mushroom gravy. I think the best way to eat them is the next day, hamburger-style in a sandwich with Dijon mustard, homemade zucchini relish or dill pickles, a few leaves of crisp lettuce, your cheese of choice, or tzatziki.

Substitute soybeans with other dried white beans, such as lima, great northern, or navy beans.

Lili Sullivan

Cook, Merrill House; Educator, The Waring House
Lili has been committed to the organic & Slow Food movements in Ontario for over twenty years.

I immigrated to Canada in 1968. I was born in Sweden, but my family is from Yugoslavia. ⁊ My parents worked, so by ten I did all the cooking at home. I was intensely into cookbooks and baking and cooking, and my Italian neighbours showed me how to can tomatoes and make cardiac-arrest lasagna layered with mortadella and hard-boiled eggs. I liked it, but we didn't go to restaurants and I didn't know you could be a chef. ⁊ I went to McMaster University to be an accountant. And my sister's first husband's cousin graduated from George Brown and went to Halifax to be a chef. And I thought, "Wow, I don't have to go to France to be a chef." So I moved to Toronto and went to George Brown. I'm still a numbers person though, so my food costing is great. ⁊ Growing up, we only shopped at the butcher. My father hunted and fished. My mother made bread. We ate what was in season. I'm sure everybody did in the seventies—there was less selection in the grocery store. No matter how poor we were, we didn't have processed food; we always had real cheese, real bread, and meat. We lived Slow Food. That's how I was raised, so I always hope that my employers will let me continue trying to be seasonal in my cooking. ⁊ I met Michael at the Auberge du Pommier in Toronto, in 1989. We hung out for a year, but I wouldn't date somebody I worked with. Then, when I realized I was going to be the sous-chef, I told him he had to quit or I wouldn't date him. Because otherwise I was going to be his boss. So he quit and they promoted me to sous-chef. We married a year later. ⁊ I'd burned out and I wanted to stop cooking. My son was at this daycare, so I ended up cooking there. It was a good break. Prior to that, I was at the Rebel House, a from-the-farm pub. We only served local beers, local wine—this was twenty-five years ago. I was part of Feast of Fields, and Knives and Forks, the organic advocates. I used everything from the farm. ⁊ We moved to the County in 2004 because Michael wanted to raise our kids in the country, but I wasn't sure about it. Now, I love the County. I would never go back to the city. I enjoy the extra time we spend chatting with the farmers and picking stuff up. ⁊ I'm currently doing breakfast for the Merrill House and teaching workshops at the Waring House's Cookery School. I don't sit very well, but at some point I'm going to slow down.

CHICKEN & ASPARAGUS TERRINE

4 tsp powdered gelatin

2 tbsp cold water

½ cup clear chicken stock

2 tbsp sherry

3½ oz sliced prosciutto

1 lb chicken thighs, boneless and skinless, poached and sliced lengthwise

16–20 spears asparagus, depending on thickness, blanched to tender-crisp

¼ cup mixed fresh herbs, minced (parsley, tarragon, chives)

kosher salt and freshly ground black pepper

chives to garnish

Add chicken, any spices you'd like to use, 1½ tablespoons salt, and enough water to cover chicken by 1 inch to a pot. Over medium heat, cover pot and bring liquid to a very low simmer. Lower heat and cook until cooked through (about 15 minutes).

Trim woody ends of asparagus. Bring a stockpot filled with 2 inches of salted water to a boil. Add asparagus and cover. Cook until bright green and tender-crisp, about 3 to 4 minutes. Remove the asparagus, place on tea towels, and pat dry.

In a small bowl, stir together gelatin and water and set aside. Heat stock, then add 1 ladle of hot stock into the gelatin; whisk together, then pour back into the stock and whisk together. Stir in sherry; season with salt and pepper. Take off heat and set aside.

Line a 12 x 2 x 2-inch loaf pan (or terrine mould) with a generous length of plastic wrap so the sides overhang the edge. Line the inside with the prosciutto, leaving some to hang over the edge. Reserve 2 slices of prosciutto for the top.

Pour a small amount of stock into bottom of pan, and fit a layer of chicken evenly together on bottom, covering completely. Place a layer of asparagus over the chicken, season lightly with salt and pepper, pour more stock over the top, then sprinkle with half the herbs. Repeat with another exact layer, then end with a third layer of chicken on top.

Use the side of your hand to gently press the chicken. Pour remaining stock across top of the terrine. Place remaining prosciutto lengthwise across the top; fold overhanging prosciutto over top. Fold overhanging wrap to cover neatly. Put in fridge on a tray to set until firm, about 1 hour.

Cut a piece of cardboard to fit perfectly on top of terrine and cover with a light weight, like an egg carton, to chill overnight. Keep terrine well chilled. Turn out from the pan, then slice with sharp knife to serve, with chives, baguette slices, and crisp greens.

Michael Sullivan

Chef, Merrill House

Michael has cooked in some of Toronto's finest kitchens, including Auberge du Pommier &
The Fifth.

I only knew the County as the sign for Sandbanks Provincial Park that we zipped past on the drive from Toronto to Montreal. Then, in 2004, a friend told me about an inn that my old co-workers, Amy and Edward Schubert, were opening in Picton. ¶ I grew up in the country. We knew the kids were going to get exposed to city life as they got older, but they might never get the rural experience. We thought this was a good place to raise our family. And suddenly the door was open. ¶ Amy and Edward gave me a tour of the Merrill Inn. It was a nice place. They were good business people, and I knew them as very decent people. But the kitchen was in terrible shape. It was basically a household kitchen with one four-burner stove and a half-size electric convection oven. And that was it. ¶ But I could cook anywhere. We quickly got another stove and to this day we only have two stoves. We manage output with good menu design. And I show up at 11:00 a.m. every day to prepare as much as possible. ¶ I was a sous-chef early, but I didn't want to be a chef until I was almost thirty-five, forty. I wasn't prepared for it. I didn't want to lead people, to tell people what to do. ¶ A menu should reflect a chef's personality, and the way they execute food is a reflection of their personality and training. If you're assigned to have to interpret somebody else's menu or execute their menu, it can be stifling. ¶ I've always cooked in the French tradition. When I was coming up as a chef, every place I worked at, that's how everyone cooked. ¶ I've been here at the Merrill going on sixteen years. It sold in 2018 to Jordan Martin. He wanted to narrow the dining room's focus to a Burgundian style. And the general manager, Christophe, is a wonderful resource for me because he's from Dijon, the capital of Burgundy. So Jordan sent me to France, to see what France was like, so I could see certain regional differences for myself. Everyone has preconceived notions about what a place is going to be like, and damned if I wasn't wrong about some things. But I was pretty spot-on with my French cuisine. I've worked with Marc Thuet, Didier Leroy—it's in their blood. I've been lucky to work with pretty good chefs. ¶ The best part of my day is when there's nobody around. First thing when you get in and it's quiet, or conversely, turning the fan off at the end of the night. You know, there's a lot going on in a cook's mind.

STEAK TARTARE

12 oz beef tenderloin

2 tbsp capers, finely chopped

1 tbsp sour cornichons (gherkins), finely chopped

2 tbsp shallots, finely minced

1 tsp Dijon mustard

1 tsp sherry vinegar

1 tsp ketchup

1 tsp Worcestershire sauce or more to taste

a dash of Tabasco sauce

2 tbsp fresh parsley, chopped

4 quail egg yolks

kosher salt and freshly ground black pepper to taste

Dice tenderloin into ¼-inch cubes with very sharp knife. Keep beef as cold as possible at all times.

Put beef into bowl and add remaining ingredients except the quail yolks. Gently fold the ingredients into the beef, until thoroughly mixed. Garnish ingredients in the beef may be increased or decreased to taste. Keep beef in refrigerator until ready to serve.

If serving right away, shape the mixture into 4 patties and place each on plate. Top each beef patty with raw quail yolk. Serve sprinkled with chopped chives, crostini, and a small dressed green salad.

Recipe makes 4 appetizer servings.

Glenn Symons

Winemaker/Cheesemaker, Lighthall Vineyards
A small, proud, low-volume & high-quality winery that also makes cheese.

I was born in North Bay. I'm Franco-Ontarian. I first learned English from *Sesame Street*. I went into pharmacy at University of Toronto, then did an MBA at the University of Ottawa. I stayed in pharmacy, bought a big store, and focused on nursing homes and retirement homes. ¶ I always made wine at home from everything, from fruit, from kits. You have to start somewhere. And I've been collecting wine since I was legally allowed to, so I've got a good collection. I did a sommelier program while I was in Ottawa, and that's where I learned about Prince Edward County. ¶ I had a heart attack at thirty-six. When I got out of the hospital, I put a For Sale sign on the door of the pharmacy. ¶ We always had a vegetable farm growing up. I didn't have any direct experience with agriculture, but I always loved the concept of putting something in the ground and having it become something completely different. So I decided to take that to the next level and make wine. ¶ The science behind winemaking is critical. You can't make good wine without a scientific approach. I've always said that wine is an artistic expression of scientific principle. My chemistry background helped put all that stuff together. ¶ Lighthall was originally planted in 2001. I took over in 2008, and 2009 was the first year we kept the fruit here. Before I took over, they were selling the fruit to Huff Estates. There's no money in growing fruit in the County unless you can add value to it, and there's no better way to add value than to ferment it. ¶ In 2008, I did an entire harvest with winemaker Fred Picard at Huff. Had I not done that, it would have taken me twenty years to understand how and what has to happen to make what we make. ¶ Cheese was the same premise: I started making cheese at home by watching YouTube. The first year we made cheese commercially here, I was making it at a bed and breakfast in Bloomfield because they had a commercial kitchen and I didn't. So once a week, we closed down here and made cheese. ¶ Wine is the reason I'm here, so wine will always be the basis of this business. But I love making cheese. It's very artisanal. It's very hands-on. So is the winemaking, but the scale is different now. Case in point, we added three new 10,000-litre tanks this year. I've lived in apartments smaller than one of those tanks. The wine has taken on a life of its own, whereas the cheese is very much still under my control. ¶ It's super-cheesy, but if you do what you love, you don't work a day in your life. This isn't a job. It's my life. This was never meant to be a hobby. ¶ For my final project in my MBA, I did an analysis of opening a new winery. It's not a good investment. And I still did it, knowing full well there is no way to get rich off a winery. It's really about passion. I live this all day, every day.

Glenn Symons (left) with Chris Thompson, assistant winemaker

HARVEST CHOUCROUTE

1 head of garlic,
roasted and peeled

8 oz pancetta

1 large jar (796 ml)
sauerkraut (without wine)

1 large white or yellow onion,
chopped

½ bottle (1½ cups) white Alsatian
wine for the pot; other half to
drink before dinner

1 lb favourite sausages; make
sure to include a 6" peeled and
quartered kielbasa

caraway seeds to your liking

fresh ground pepper to
your liking

To roast the garlic, preheat your oven (or toaster oven) to 400°F. Peel and discard the papery outer layers of the garlic bulb. Leave skins intact on individual garlic cloves. Use a sharp knife to trim ¼-inch from top of cloves. Cover entire garlic head with aluminum foil and place the garlic head on a baking sheet, trimmed side up. Bake for 30 to 40 minutes or until cloves are soft when pressed. Let cool, then squeeze roasted garlic out of skins.

To fry pancetta, heat a large frying pan over medium heat. Add pancetta and cook until browned and crisp, about 5 minutes per side. Briefly drain fried pancetta on a paper towel-lined plate.

To assemble choucroute, combine garlic, pancetta, sauerkraut, onion, wine, and spices in a Dutch oven. Add sausages on top and bake at 250°F for 2 hours, covered.

Serve with boiled potatoes, with melted raclette cheese on the side, and a fresh baguette for shits and giggles. Serve with at least one more bottle of the same wine that was in the pot, for accompaniment.

Ed & Sandi Taylor

Farmers, Honey Wagon Farms
A farm run by retirees focused on growing regular & specialty vegetables without the use of herbicides, fungicides, or pesticides.

I've always been impressed that seeds will produce all the food you need to live. It's miraculous. A carrot seed is so small you can't really hold it in your fingers. And then a hundred days later it produces this beautiful, nutritious, lifesaving thing. ¶ There's so much going on in the field. And when the food's ready, it'll just sit there and wait until it's harvested. If you leave it long enough, it will freeze and die and then turn back into earth. Or, in the case of parsnips, they just get better, because they can stay in the field all winter and they're actually tastier first thing in the spring. ¶ It's challenging to get chefs or owners to think in January and February about what they might need in August, September, and October. But that's the timeline we have. With that said, we have a pretty good idea of what they'll want. I don't cook in the kitchen with them, but I might as well, because I pay close attention to their ordering patterns. ¶ I really like chefs to come to the farm and walk in the field with me. I don't say too much, just have them walk by my tomatoes, okra, purple cabbage, savoy cabbage. They don't have to commit to it, but I'll earmark produce for them so that I can be ready. ¶ We only do greens for personal use. We're heavy on potatoes, heavy on squash, and we do pretty well a bit of everything else. French filet beans and snap peas and broccoli and cauliflower. ¶ Our idea of local is that Prince Edward County is local. When we're at the Kingston market and someone asks if our produce is local, we say, "No, it's not, it's from Prince Edward County." It's just an hour away, but for us, local means the community where the food is grown. ¶ Sandi and I do almost everything ourselves. We only hire when we absolutely need another person. People are surprised to hear I'm seventy-five. But I used to work as a vice-principal. Sandi was a kindergarten teacher. We don't want to supervise people again. And I don't want to grow and sell more stuff to pay the extra expense. We do hire, but only when we absolutely have to, because someone has to ride on the machine behind the tractor and someone has to drive the tractor. So we just do selective five-hour slots here and there with people we know can do it. And we pay them well because we want them back. ¶ What's closing in on me is the reality of time. Our farming practices may have to evolve to accommodate our age. We don't use any sprays or chemicals or anything to kill weeds, except physical labour. When we have an 800-foot row of beets, well, we both weed it. ¶ Sandi's been actively involved really since the start. She's great at the farm stand and the markets. And if anything is finessed in regard to the farm, all the signage, how we lay stuff out, all the seasonal decorations, that's all Sandi. ¶ We weren't lucky enough to have kids, so we divert a significant amount of profits to charities. Kingston General saved my life twelve years ago, so we give to them. We donate to local food banks and other organizations. And we give away food too. Last year, we ended up growing way too much, and we must've given close to 4,000 pounds of potatoes and squash to food banks.

KOHLRABI & CARROT SLAW

Salad

1 large kohlrabi, peeled, stems trimmed off, grated

2 medium carrots, peeled and grated

½ red onion, sliced

4 tbsp chopped cilantro (optional)

¼ cup golden raisins or dried sweetened cranberries (optional)

Dressing

¼ cup mayonnaise

1 tbsp apple cider vinegar, unfiltered

1 tbsp maple syrup
(adjust quantity to desired taste)

1 tsp salt

> By substituting celeriac, this can also double as celeriac slaw. The dressing has a bite, and a combo of sweet syrup and tart vinegar; adjust the ingredient quantities to suit your own taste.

In a large bowl, combine the kohlrabi, carrots, onion, cilantro, raisins or cranberries (if using).

In a smaller bowl, whisk together the mayonnaise, cider vinegar, maple syrup, and salt.

Pour the dressing over the slaw and mix fully to coat. Chill several hours before serving.

Samantha Valdivia

Chef, La Condesa

A colourful restaurant that celebrates the beautiful cuisine & culture of Mexico.

I'm from Mexico, Cancún. Believe it or not, people live there. ¶ I always liked baking because I liked travelling. I would bake to raise money and travel. I didn't really think you could make money cooking. But when I came to Canada, I got a job in a Mexican restaurant after walking in off the street and very quickly got good at it. ¶ I started with Chipotle, which is a completely different restaurant ideology than anywhere else. I learned about the food business in a reverse way—I managed food first, which helped me understand all the number things, and then I started cooking after. The fast-food world actually gave me good roads to understand a P&L. After five years, I changed jobs and began actually having fun in the kitchen. ¶ Preparing tacos can be incredibly challenging. In a normal restaurant, for a table of four, it's four dishes and then you're done. At La Condesa, it's probably thirteen or fourteen dishes. I try to send food as fast as I can to make sure everyone has something. But at the same time, I'm making sure they've finished eating and it's not too early. This system of taco serving, it's chaotic. I don't look at one chit. I look at the whole board—it's like playing Tetris. ¶ When I travel, I'm definitely looking at food. I try to balance out the culture, the food. But there are trips where I go to Mexico just to eat. ¶ I found out about the County four years ago. A friend invited me here for Thanksgiving dinner at their house. I took a cab from the train station, and the entire time it was so picturesque it felt like I was in a movie. The County sucks you in and doesn't let you go. ¶ We get most of our veggies from Fiddlehead Farm. We order them a year in advance because they plant specific tomatillos for us. It's just like Mexican food but grown in the County. Even though our restaurant is located on the other side of the County, I stayed committed to them because they went the extra mile for us. You have to commit. ¶ I wasn't planning on opening a restaurant. The opportunity just came up, and I couldn't say no. It was a built restaurant. You turn the key and it's ready; we had a month to flip and open. And I thought, "There goes all our savings for our home. We're opening a restaurant."

Top: Samantha Valdivia with sous-chef Rizal Adam
Bottom: Matthew Gilsenan, beverage director

CHILES RELLENOS

Poblano Pepper

6 large fresh poblano peppers

6 egg whites

1½ cups Oaxacan cheese
(or 3-year-old white cheddar, or
mozzarella), grated

all-purpose flour (or corn flour
or gluten-free flour), enough for
coating chiles

Tomato Broth

12 Roma tomatoes, halved

1 white onion, quartered

6 garlic cloves

5 whole allspice

4 whole black peppercorns

½ bunch fresh cilantro, chopped

kosher salt

vegetable oil

Heat pan on medium heat. Roast poblanos until charred on all sides.

Place poblanos in container and cover with lid for 10 minutes, allowing them to steam and loosen their skins. Peel off the skins and make a small incision in the middle of each poblano. Remove seeds and veins, keeping shape intact. Stuff each poblano with cheese and refrigerate for 10 minutes.

While poblanos are chilling in fridge, place tomatoes, onion, and garlic in blender and blend until completely smooth. Strain salsa through fine strainer. Place strained salsa in saucepan on medium-low heat. Add allspice and black pepper and bring to a simmer. Skim off any froth that forms on top.

Remove poblanos from fridge. Place egg whites in a bowl and whip until they have soft peaks. Heat a large pan with an inch of oil.

Coat each poblano with flour and then cover with egg white batter. Carefully place each chile, one at a time, in the hot oil and cook until golden on both sides.

To serve, place each chile in a shallow bowl and ladle with sauce to cover. Garnish with cilantro.

You can also roast poblanos over a gas stove's open flame, turning to char and soften evenly before placing in a container and covering with lid to steam and loosen their skins.

Brian & Jane Walt

Farmers, Walt's Sugar Shack

Brian started the Sugar Shack in 1999 on land cared for by four generations of the Walt family.

We met when Brian hired Jane as a forensic accountant. We only started farming three years ago, but Brian had always wanted to be a farmer. Our friend David lost his son at the age of fourteen, and he told Brian that if there's anything he wanted to do with the kids, to hurry up and get at it. So we got horses and ponies for the kids. And when the kids moved out, we bought two cows because we'd always wanted them. And that's where it started with the animals. ¶ We got pigs two summers ago because we needed a thousand pounds of sausages at the Sugar Shack—we use a thousand pounds for our pancake breakfasts during Maple in the County. ¶ We had a hard time figuring out what to feed them to produce good sausage. Then we discovered that one of the breweries was having trouble getting rid of used barley. A farmer had day-old vegetables they needed to get rid of. Another place needed their cover crop taken off. It all works perfectly as pig food. ¶ We're like agricultural recycling. There's so much stuff that's wasted otherwise. And the pigs love it. It's good business sense too, because it saves us from buying tons of feed. And the farmers and brewers are able to create less waste. ¶ You have to like the animals or you're not going to enjoy farming. We really look forward to feeding the baby calves. They're like toddlers. You have to pay attention to them, you have to give them a good life. ¶ For processing, we take them to the Amish boys at Hastings Meat Market. One of the reasons we like to go there is that it takes ten seconds. It's very quick, very humane. But it's the hardest part of the whole deal. ¶ The whole enterprise has grown faster than we ever intended. A few times in the last year, it's been very difficult keeping up to demand. At one point, we had 10,000 people at the shack in two days. Ninety percent of them were young families. They're willing to spend the money they have on what they want. They want natural sugar products. But this is what we wanted. And we've got a lot of room to grow. ¶ We're a family business. We believe in building relationships with other local people. And we do our best to bring a high quality to the table.

ROSEMARY MAPLE GLAZED NUTS

5 cups unsalted mixed nuts

4 tbsp butter

4 tbsp Walt's Sugar
Shack maple syrup

2 tbsp crushed dried rosemary
(or 4 tbsp chopped fresh
rosemary)

1 tbsp coarse black pepper

2 tbsp crunchy sea salt

Preheat oven to 350°F. Spread parchment paper over a large baking sheet.

Melt butter in a saucepan and add maple syrup and all the seasonings.

In a large bowl, combine nuts and butter mixture, and mix thoroughly.

Pour nut mixture onto the prepared baking sheet; spread evenly. Bake for 15 to 20 minutes, depending on how darkly roasted you like them, stirring every 5 minutes. Remove from oven and place baking sheet on a cooling rack.

After 20 minutes, stir the mixture again, then allow it to cool completely. Enjoy!

Store cooled nuts in an airtight container.

Henry Willis

Baker, Humble Bread

A small bakeshop that produces high-quality naturally leavened breads.

I'm a math and science guy, and baking naturally leavened bread is mostly scientific. Every time I bake, I'm always amazed to see what flour, water, and salt can create. ¶ We lived in Scarborough for seven years, where we built a wood-burning oven in our backyard. Starting a micro bread-baking business there made me realize this was a passion and I wanted to continue it, but in a rural environment. I wanted to focus on selling at farmers' markets, and looked for communities that were within driving distance to good year-round markets that we could be part of. We fell in love with the County years ago, having come camping with the kids, and found it met all our needs and more. ¶ I only bake using natural leavening techniques. I don't use any commercial yeast—it's not needed. Flour. Water. Salt. I only source the best quality flour, since naturally leavened baking is not a forgiving process. It's a craft. ¶ I take it for granted now that I only bake in a wood-fired oven, but the combination of the natural leaven and the oven makes very unique products. A regular oven bakes from the outside in, which causes the bread to lose quite a bit of moisture, whereas a wood-fired oven penetrates evenly and intensely using radiant energy. A standard loaf for bread in a standard commercial oven takes thirty-five or forty minutes to bake. My loaves bake in as little as eight or nine minutes. The radiant energy my oven produces is huge. ¶ I'm a one-man show. I've modelled everything I do—my schedule, my oven, my bakeshop—to work for me, one man. ¶ I'm at the point now where I have a great relationship with my oven. I know what to expect. I have many loaves to bake before I can go to sleep each night, and they all have to be delicious! ¶ I think naturally leavened bread, baked in a wood-fired oven, is the highest order of bread in the world. Making healthy, digestible, and delicious bread for our community is why I love what I do.

RAISIN RYE FRENCH TOAST BAKE

Any of Humble Bread's breads are awesome for French toast. I usually use raisin; however, I've also used Wilson Road Rye, multigrain, as well as 100 percent red fife. Tossing and leaving it to sit overnight is a must—the bread needs time to absorb the egg mixture. It's quick to put together at night, and then in the morning, after baking, you have a delicious warm breakfast that makes the house smell lovely.

10 cups Humble Bread Raisin Rye, or substitute with any quality sourdough bread, with or without raisins

8 large eggs

2½ cups whole milk, or substitute with a mix of milk and cream

¼ cup sugar

½ cup brown sugar

1 tbsp vanilla extract

2 tsp cinnamon

1 tsp nutmeg

Cut bread into 1-inch cubes. In a large bowl, combine the rest of the ingredients. Stir in the cubed bread. Refrigerate overnight, stirring as often as you'd like.

In the morning, preheat oven to 360°F. Butter a 13 x 9-inch pan. Pour the bread and egg mixture into the pan.

Bake 30 minutes, spin 180°, and bake for another 20 minutes (about 50 minutes total) or until the centre is no longer wet.

I like the top to be a little crunchy; after about 45 minutes, remove the pan from the oven, turn broil on high, and place the pan back in the oven for a few minutes with the door slightly ajar. If you do this, be mindful—it can burn quickly!

Natalie Wollenberg

Co-owner, The County Canteen & 555 Brewing Co.

The Canteen offers Ontario craft beer & pub fare; 555 is a brewery featuring wood-fired pizza.

In 2003, we'd just moved to Perth, Australia, and my husband, Drew, decided making beer was a good idea. He started off with home-brew kits, and then all of a sudden he really got into it, sanitizing and MacGyvering everything. You'd roll up the garage door on weekends and he'd be brewing, wearing his Leafs jersey. ¶ We thought about starting a brewery in Australia, but Drew was a bit homesick. We came back to help Drew's parents settle into their new house in 2012. And that's when we decided to move to the County. Who wouldn't want to move here? It took us two years. ¶ The County Canteen opened on June 24, 2015, a year and two days after we arrived. It was a whirlwind, even with a lot of people helping us. There was nothing else like it in Picton, so we didn't know what to expect. When we opened, it was the biggest tornado I've ever been in. We had to hire so many people so quickly because we did not expect the response. ¶ Like a lot of restaurant owners do, we went in incredibly green. Initially, the Canteen was going to be a brew pub with snacks. But we listened to the advice of other chefs and cooks and people in hospitality, and we made changes, because we realized that if we stuck to our original idea, we'd be broke. ¶ When we were brewing out of the Canteen, we had no room. Drew made it work; he's amazing at being able to do that. But we got to the stage where our beer would be sold out within thirty-six hours. There was no storage. It's a really old building. One day, Drew said, "Let's go for a walk." And so we went for a walk up the road to where the brewery is now. And he said, "Look at that patio. This is a beer garden." It was empty at the time. And so we spoke to the landlord, and then all of a sudden it was off and running. 555 opened in 2017, two years after the Canteen was born. ¶ It was a huge leap to have two places. Especially while you're going through all those stumbling things like you normally do with business and hospitality, and processes and staff, and what you're serving and food and beer and trying to keep things in stock. ¶ Our staff provide us with a lot of inspiration. They all get why we're doing what we're doing. And we like being able to make changes to the menu by listening to the customers. That's how we came up with the new veggie burger at the Canteen. One of the kitchen guys and I worked on it. People suggested black beans, beetroot. It took us five tries. On the fourth try, the burger was really good, but something was missing. Chris Byrne, the vegan chef, happened to be at the bar with us. He told us to add brown rice and we'd have a winner. And that's how we got the recipe. I love that kind of collaboration. ¶ Cooking's always been one thing I've really loved. I love that people enjoy what I cook for them. That's why I'm sharing my recipe for puttanesca—it's Drew's favourite meal. And that's why I love making it.

PUTTANESCA SAUCE WITH ROASTED EGGPLANT

4 tbsp olive oil

1 medium eggplant, diced

2 large shallots, chopped

4 garlic cloves, minced

½ tsp red pepper flakes

5–7 anchovies

1 can (796 ml)
whole peeled tomatoes

¼ cup red wine

200 g kalamata olives,
pitted and roughly chopped

2 tbsp capers

4 sprigs oregano,
coarsely chopped

¼ cup chopped flat parsley

1 package (450 g) spaghetti

salt for pasta water

Parmesan to taste

Preheat oven to 425°F.

In a large bowl, toss the eggplant with half the olive oil, and season with salt and pepper to taste. Bake in a single layer on a large baking sheet, for about 20 minutes, stirring occasionally, or until starting to brown on all sides.

Meanwhile, in a large pot over medium heat, heat the remaining olive oil. Add shallots and garlic and sauté for 2 minutes or until softened. Add red pepper flakes, anchovies, tomatoes, red wine, olives, capers, and oregano. Simmer for about 15 minutes or until sauce thickens slightly. Add chopped parsley and roasted eggplant; stir into sauce to combine.

While sauce is simmering, boil water for spaghetti; add a pinch of salt. Cook spaghetti until al dente and drain. Serve pasta topped with puttanesca sauce, sprinkled with additional chopped parsley, liberal shavings of Parmesan, a healthy glass of wine, and baguette.

Chris Wylie

Chef, The Manse Boutique Inn & Spa

Chris sources the finest local ingredients to create memorable meals for the Manse's guests.

My first introduction to the kitchen was washing dishes at a Greek restaurant in Belleville, Ontario, when I was fourteen. I worked there for five years and slowly made my way to line cook while still in high school. After high school, I wanted to expand my horizons, so I tried to move out of the restaurant industry and into construction. But I kept being lured back to the kitchen. ¶ During a semester in college, I took a placement at the Briars, a resort and spa in Jacksons Point, Ontario. From the excellent chef and staff there, I learned the true meaning of cooking from scratch, of using farm-fresh local ingredients. I realized there was actual science and chemistry and skill involved in cooking. The entire experience was an awakening, and food became my passion. ¶ I worked in Toronto for a few years, and then a friend asked me to come be a chef up in Magnetawan, just north of Huntsville, where he was starting a new restaurant. Being able to design my own menu, kitchen, and dining room was a dream, and I was able to hone my skills and develop my technique. And that's where I met my wife Kathleen. ¶ We moved back to Belleville where I became the executive chef of a locally owned Southern smokehouse. Experimenting with different cuts of meat and smoking was an enjoyable and rewarding experience, as it takes time and patience. ¶ Three years later, I made the move to Picton to take up the position of head chef and assistant innkeeper at the Manse, in partnership with my wife. Running the Manse has given me the opportunity to make lasting connections with local producers and farmers in the County. I offer breakfast for our overnight guests, picnic lunches, multi-course dinners, and we do the occasionally wedding and family reunion. ¶ The Manse is private dining, and I send out my menu before my guests arrive. I love receiving their requests and exclamations of anticipation. Being a small location, I always make every meal from scratch. I love being able to provide an amazing experience.

CURRIED CARROT GINGER SOUP

¼ cup vegetable oil

1 white onion, chopped

1 head of garlic, peeled
and chopped

1 4" piece fresh ginger (no need to
peel), chopped

2 tbsp curry powder

3 lbs carrots, sliced (additional to
those in braised carrot stock)

3½ cups store-bought
vegetable broth

braised carrot stock
(see recipe below)

1 can (400 ml) full-fat coconut milk

salt and pepper to taste

In a deep pot, heat oil over medium heat, and add onion and a pinch of salt. Reduce heat to low and sweat onion, stirring occasionally, for about 5 minutes or until translucent.

Increase heat to medium and add garlic and ginger. Cook for about 3 to 5 minutes, stirring occasionally. Add curry powder and stir for about 2 to 3 minutes or until toasted and aromatic.

Add carrots and stir until coated. Add vegetable stock and braised carrot stock. Cook over low heat, covered, for about 30 minutes or until carrots are tender. Remove from heat and stir in coconut milk. Season with salt to taste.

In a blender or food processor (or using an immersion blender), purée soup in batches until smooth. Strain mixture through a fine-meshed sieve into another pot and reheat.

Serve sprinkled with microgreens or fresh thyme, salt, pepper, and a drizzle of pumpkin seed oil.

BRAISED CARROT STOCK

3 lbs carrots, sliced

1 cup each water and
orange juice (enough to just
submerge the carrots)

2 tbsp butter

honey

salt

Preheat oven to 350°F. In an ovenproof pan, add carrots and cover with water, orange juice, butter, a drizzle of honey, and a good sprinkle of salt.

Cover surface of carrots with parchment paper and bake for 1½ hours or until carrots are tender. Strain carrot stock and reserve for making curried carrot ginger soup. Serve remaining braised carrots with salt, pepper, and a little butter.

This can be made a few days ahead, if desired.

If using organic carrots, simply scrub them with water. Conventional carrots should be peeled before cooking. Pumpkin seed oil is available at most health food and specialty stores.

Hidde Zomer

Chef, Flame + Smith
A sustainably minded restaurant that embraces the exciting art of wood-fire cooking.

I loved food at a young age. My mom and grandmother were good cooks. My dad could cook too, so, growing up, I spent a lot of time cooking. ¶ My first job was in a Chinese restaurant working as a dishwasher. It was a beautiful, high-end place in Haarlem, Netherlands, and it was the first time it ever hit me that cooking is a pretty cool job. These Chinese chefs yelling at each other, stuff flying around really fast—it was such a hectic, wild environment. Seeing them cook, actually creating something, it was the first time I really fell in love with it. ¶ Cooking is about family and sharing food. At the restaurant, I don't cook the way I do at my house, but it's still about representing what you do at home. It has to feel natural. ¶ My wife Sarah and I always wanted to own a restaurant. We had a conversation about a ten-year plan to open a restaurant in the countryside, somewhere we feel close to terroir and farmland. ¶ In the beginning, we were a little naive. We wanted to find a farm with a barn we could convert into a restaurant—and then reality kicked in. If you're on farmland, how do you operate your business? If you're on a well, can the restaurant function properly? How will you heat the barn? So the dream had to shift. ¶ We were getting closer to the end of the ten years. So in 2018, I left my job in Toronto and moved to the County full-time. And that was the scariest moment of my life. We had a three-year-old kid and another one on the way. And I was building a restaurant from the ground up. ¶ Starting a restaurant from scratch is a pain. But it's also amazing because I can shape it exactly how I want it to be. ¶ I couldn't be happier with the team that we built. We do some really big nights, and it's tough to cook your heart out every day. But the expectation is high, and that's something we have to live up to. ¶ We're humble about the fact that we have to create a memorable experience for all these guests. But also, it's very fantastic and fun to work the fire into the menu. It's also just great to have a real connection with my guests. ¶ The beaches in the County remind me of Holland. The dunes are the only nature they have there. And the vegetation is the same, the silver-and-green plants, those trees and the water. I feel right at home here.

WOOD-FIRED BELGIAN ENDIVE

I have many fond memories of this classic Dutch dish. My mother used to make this often in the colder winter months as a casserole. It's great served family-style on a midweek day, and perfect as a side dish paired with a Sunday roast.

Before we opened Flame + Smith, my mother was visiting from the Netherlands and made this for my family one evening. We were still in menu development, and I thought it would be a great side dish, so I decided to try to cook this in our wood-burning oven. It worked perfectly and quickly became one of our most popular side dishes. This dish works just as well in a gas or convection oven. This recipe will serve 4 people.

Endive

8 heads large, firm Belgian endives

8 slices good-quality cooked ham from your local butcher shop or deli

3 oz grated hard cheeses for sprinkling (Gruyère, Swiss, and sharp white aged cheddar are best)

Mornay Sauce

3 tbsp unsalted butter

3 tbsp all-purpose flour

1½ cups 3.25% milk

1 bay leaf

1 tbsp whole black peppercorns

2 sprigs thyme

1 cup Spanish onion, large dice

2 garlic cloves

1½ oz grated Swiss or Gruyère (about ⅓ cup)

1½ oz grated aged white cheddar (about ⅓ cup)

kosher salt

Preheat the oven to 350°F on convection, or 375°F on a gas oven.

Start by making the Mornay sauce, as this will take about 15 minutes. Alternatively, the Mornay can be made ahead and holds up to 5 days refrigerated in an airtight container.

This sauce starts as a béchamel, and when adding the cheeses it becomes a Mornay. All béchamel sauces start with making a blond roux, which helps thicken the sauce and prevents it from splitting. Mornay sauce is very versatile and great for many dishes, such as macaroni and cheese, scalloped potatoes, and cauliflower gratin.

Melt butter in a 1-quart heavy-bottomed sauce pot on low heat; do not brown the butter. Once melted, add flour and mix using a spatula until well incorporated. The roux should have the consistency of a soft cake batter. Cook the roux gently for 5 minutes on low heat, stirring every minute or so to prevent browning.

Heat up the milk separately with bay leaf, peppercorns, and thyme; steep for 5 minutes at a low simmer. Strain the milk through a fine mesh sieve and discard the solids. Incorporate the hot milk slowly into the pot with the cooked roux, adding a couple ladles at a time and stirring vigorously with a spatula or small whisk until all the milk is incorporated into the roux. Cook while stirring to prevent the bottom of the pot from burning for a few more minutes. Whisk in the grated cheeses. Continue to cook the béchamel for a few minutes. Season with kosher salt to taste.

Cut the endives in half lengthwise and remove a little of the brown bottom part of the heads with a sharp paring knife. Lay slices of ham on a clean counter or baking tray, and wrap 2 half-pieces (one halved endive per ham slice) tightly in the ham.

Take a casserole dish and spread out some Mornay sauce until the bottom of the casserole is covered, about ¼-inch thick. Lay the 8 ham-wrapped endives in the casserole and add a touch more Mornay on top.

Sprinkle grated cheeses on top and place in preheated oven for 15 to 20 minutes. When ready, the cheese and ham should have a beautiful golden-brown colour, the sauce should be bubbling, and it will have a fantastic aroma of caramelized ham and cheese. You can use the broil setting on your oven to create a deeper-coloured caramelized crust if desired.